Benjamin Harrison

Benjamin Harrison

by

ELISABETH P. MYERS

REILLY & LEE BOOKS
a division of Henry Regnery Company
CHICAGO, ILLINOIS

Photographs supplied by
HISTORICAL PICTURES SERVICE · CHICAGO

1521621

Contents

No Hat but His Own

BENJAMIN HARRISON, the twenty-third President of the United States, was the great-grandson of a signer of the Declaration of Independence, the grandson of a President, and the son of a congressman.

His earliest really vivid memory was of the "goings on" during the campaign of 1840, which preceded the election of his grandfather, William Henry Harrison, to the highest office in the land. It was no wonder they impressed the seven-year-old boy. That campaign was quite possibly the noisiest, jolliest one ever conducted. It was certainly the first one to make wide use of party slogans, party insignia, and party songs.

Ironically, the impetus for the most appealing of these came from a supporter of Harrison's Democratic opponent, Martin Van Buren. On the front page of a widely read pro-Van Buren newspaper, an uninformed Baltimore journalist sneered at the Whigs' homespun hero: "Give Granny Harrison a barrel of hard cider and settle a pension of two thousand a year on him and, my word for it, he will sit the remainder of his days in his log cabin."

That reporter's word wasn't very reliable; Harrison's background was much more aristocratic than Van Buren's. He was the son of a landed Virginia gentleman, Benjamin, the Declaration signer. He grew up on the family plantation on the James River, while the War of the Revolution raged

all around him. He was ten when peace was declared, but
he continued to be educated at home by tutors until 1787.
Then, at age fourteen, he was sent to Hampden-Sidney
College, Virginia, where he undertook a pre-medical course
of study.

It was his father's wish that William Henry be a doctor,
but the boy chafed at the inactivity of constant study. He
kept hearing reports of Indian attacks in the Northwest
Territory, the frontier region between the Ohio and Mississippi rivers. He longed to do what he could to combat
the savage forces.

His graduation from college coincided with his father's
death. However, since he was not yet eighteen, William
Henry became the ward of his father's friend, the financier
of the Revolution, Robert Morris. As such, he had to defer
to his guardian's wishes. Morris was no more in favor of
his joining the army than his father had been, but their
"great and good friend," George Washington, was.

Thanks to the first President of the United States, in
November, 1791, William Henry Harrison was commissioned ensign in the first regiment of regular artillery, then
in garrison at Fort Washington, in the vicinity of Cincinnati. The following year he became aide-de-camp to the fort
commander, General Anthony Wayne.

Harrison paid close attention to the training and instruc-
tion Wayne gave the troops regarding Indian warfare.
Aware of this, Wayne soon recommended Harrison for promotion to lieutenant and kept the young man at his side
during his powwow with the chiefs of the Six Nations in
March, 1792.

Harrison was with Wayne in his campaign in northwest
Ohio, which ended in the Battle of Fallen Timbers on
August 20, 1794. This victory ended Indian resistance in
that area for a long time. With the northwest frontier now

secure for the Americans, the upper Ohio Valley could be
settled. Harrison was rewarded for his part in the victory
by being promoted to captain and by replacing Wayne as
commander at Fort Washington when Wayne moved on
to other danger spots.

While in command at the fort, Captain Harrison met
Anna Symmes, daughter of a prominent Revolutionary
patriot. In 1787, John Cleve Symmes had bought a twenty-
mile strip of land located between the two Miamis in Ohio
Territory. On maps of that period, this strip is designated
"Symmes' Purchase." Symmes founded the town of North
Bend, and it was there in November, 1795, that Anna
Symmes became Captain Harrison's bride.

In 1798, Harrison resigned from the army to become
Secretary of the Northwest Territory and, in 1799, its first
delegate to Congress. There he helped get through the legislation that separated what is now the state of Ohio from
the Northwest Territory. All that remained was christened
Indiana Territory.

In January, 1800, when William Henry Harrison was
only twenty-eight years old, President John Adams appointed him governor of this vast newly created area. It was
a post he was to hold for twelve years, being reappointed by
Presidents Jefferson and Madison.

His position was autocratic. He was commander of the
militia. He appointed all civil officers. He sat in judgment
of all land titles, and his decision was final. He was also
general Indian agent, made all treaties, and negotiated all
payments in connection with these. By the treaties, the
southern part of the present state of Indiana and portions
of the present states of Illinois, Wisconsin, and Missouri
were opened to settlement.

It was the Indian cessions of 1809 along the Wabash
River that aroused the hostility of that "eloquent and ener-

getic" Shawnee chieftain, Tecumseh, and his brother, the Prophet. They claimed that the treaty ceding those lands was illegal, that the consent of all tribes living there had not been obtained. They threatened to form a confederation that would include all the tribes of the North as well as the Cherokees, Choctaws, Creeks, and Seminoles of the South. United, they would block the westward sweep of white settlement.

The Indians were egged on by British authorities in Canada. Great Britain had been forced by American pressure to vacate her outposts in the Great Lakes region and was still resentful. Attacks against Indiana's frontier settlements grew more and more violent, and the people begged Governor Harrison to do something.

At first he tried conciliatory measures; conferences between himself and the chieftains were held at Vincennes, the territorial capital, and again at the Indian camp. But it was no use. In the end, Harrison had to fight force with force.

In September, 1811, Harrison set off with a thousand men toward the Prophet's town, Tippecanoe, a hundred and fifty miles north of Vincennes and located on the Tippecanoe River near its confluence with the Wabash. On November 6 they arrived within a mile and a half of the village. Here they were met by Indian messengers, who said the chiefs wanted a parley. Harrison granted one for the next day, and his troops set up camp for the night.

Harrison was too wise in the ways of Indian warfare to trust the Prophet's pledge of "peace until parley." He told his men to keep their clothes on and their weapons nearby. He ordered the sentries to maintain extreme vigilance, for their lives might depend on it.

He was right. About four o'clock in the morning, a sentry saw the form of an Indian near him in the grass and fired an alarm. Said a report of the engagement: "Harrison sprang from his tent, the soldiers were on their feet, and the fight was on. The roar of musketry, the yell of savages, the groans of the wounded and dying, and the voice of the commander were all mingled."

Heavy fighting lasted most of the day, until Harrison and his men destroyed the Prophet's settlement and defeated the Indians. So ended the Battle of Tippecanoe, which earned William Henry Harrison his famous nickname and the undying gratitude of multitudes of his fellow Americans. He was to win more military laurels in the War of 1812, and afterwards to become a United States Senator, the first minister of the United States to the Republic of Colombia and, briefly, President. Nevertheless, to the people he remained their frontier hero, Old Tippecanoe.

In politics, Harrison was naturally a Federalist, the party whose policies dominated the administrations of Washington and John Adams. It was the first national political party in the United States, created after the split between Hamilton and Jefferson in Washington's Cabinet. It was somewhat authoritarian in its political theory, liberal in its interpretation of the national government's powers under the Constitution, quite the opposite of everything that the third President of the United States, Thomas Jefferson, advocated.

The Democratic Party traces its origin back to what was called "Jeffersonian democracy," but it really arose from the personal following of Andrew Jackson in the campaign of 1824. In that period it stood for frontier democracy, equality, and the abolition of special privileges. The White House under Jackson became the "People's House," and they loved the President who belonged to *them*.

"They," of course, were "Mr. and Mrs. Ordinary American." Unordinary Americans—businessmen, large landholders, anybody who had a cause of any sort to back— hated Jackson just as deeply. They felt that he was out to destroy private enterprise. They knew that their only hope

of breaking Jackson's hold on the country lay in forgetting
their differences and forming a new party.

In 1834 the Whig Party was born. Its members were of
various small party affiliations, but all were people who
blamed "King Andrew" for everything that was wrong in
the nation.

Jackson, after serving eight years as President, was quite
willing to retire to his home in Tennessee. But he was
unwilling to see his policies altered, so in 1836 he designated his Vice-president, Martin Van Buren, as heir to the
office.

The Whig coalition, unable to agree upon a single candidate, adopted the strategy of nominating candidates with
strong local followings in the hope of throwing the election
into the House. In January, 1835, Daniel Webster was nominated by the Massachusetts legislative caucus. In the same
month Hugh L. White was chosen by anti-Jacksonian
Democrats in the Tennessee legislature. The Anti-Masonic
party nominated William Henry Harrison. The Whig
candidates received 736,250 votes, Van Buren 761,549.

So Van Buren won, but he did not have an easy time in
office. Within days after his accession he was faced with a
major national depression—the Panic of 1837—which was
to bother him all during his administration.

The basic cause of the financial crash was the execution
of and opposition to Jackson's "Specie Circular" of July
11, 1836, which stated that from that day forward the government would accept only specie—gold or silver—in payment for public lands. Jackson's object was to stop the use
of paper or "land office" money (currency based on speculators' notes) by speculators and capitalists, who wanted to
buy up huge parcels of land with the aim of selling it later
for private profit.

The Circular succeeded in reducing public land sales in
the West, but it had other, far less desirable effects. It

drained specie from the East, led to hoarding, and weakened public confidence in state banks. Businesses collapsed from lack of hard money to repay loans. Food and fuel prices and rent soared. Hardship was everywhere.

Such a state of affairs made many enemies for Van Buren. Everybody wanted him to do something about the depression. Yet, no matter what he decided to do, his decision would be sure to displease some sector of the economy. He ended up "fence-sitting"—doing as little as possible, to avoid offending anyone.

One major problem was that Van Buren saw the role of the President in the life of the nation as very limited. He was a states' rights advocate, believing that the federal government had no constitutional authority to correct inequities or resolve crises.

Though to him the President was only a figurehead, he wasn't averse to making that image regal at the expense of the people. He wore what scoffers called "Fancy Nancy" clothes and rode in an olive green carriage attended by liveried footmen and pulled by horses wearing silvered harnesses. Worse, in the middle of the depression, he spent over $27,000—an enormous sum in those days—refurnishing the White House. Said one of his detractors, Pennsylvania congressman Charles Ogle: "The cost of three White House curtains alone would build at least three goodly log cabins with money to spare. There'd be enough left over to treat the folks who came to the house-raising with as much hard cider as they could stow away under the belts of their linsey-woolsey shirts."

Ogle went on to charge that the White House was no longer the "People's House," as it had been when Jackson was President. Quite the contrary. "Luxuriating in sloth and effeminacy, Van Buren reigns at the cost of the nation," Ogle said.

Whig Party leaders were quick to see what this dissatisfaction could mean for them. If they could come up with a man who would be a clear contrast to "Fancy Nancy" Van Buren, they should be able to seize the Presidency from him with ease in 1840.

Who would qualify? In the campaign of 1836, they remembered, William Henry Harrison had made much the best showing among the Whig candidates. Yet he was a genuine aristocrat, kin to many of the first families of Virginia, chosen by John Quincy Adams as the "gentleman best suited to be the first United States minister to the Republic of Colombia."

Nicholas Biddle, former president of the Bank of the United States, reminded his Whig friends that Harrison was also a famous Indian fighter. Biddle added that, though he was not a betting man, he was willing to wager that the people had not forgotten Old Tippecanoe.

To the question of what sort of platform of principles Harrison should be given to stand on, Biddle replied, "None." The only issue of the campaign would be, as he saw it, whether or not the Van Buren administration should be allowed to continue.

Accordingly, at the Whig Convention in Harrisburg, Pennsylvania, in December, 1839, Harrison was nominated for the Presidency. As his running mate the Whigs chose John Tyler. Tyler was a "disillusioned Democrat" and might be expected to draw the votes of others like himself.

"With Tippecanoe and Tyler too, we can win," the delegates assured each other.

They left the convention hall chanting that alliterative phrase, one that caught the attention of everyone who heard it. Soon people were chanting:

"The beautiful girls, God bless their souls,
souls, souls, the country through,

Will all, to a man, do all they can
for Tippecanoe and Tyler, too!"

Biddle had cautioned Harrison "to say not a single word about his principles or creed—to promise nothing." If he was called upon to speak, he was to dwell on his frontier years. To win the election, the Whigs had to attract the poor and the people who lived in the western part of the nation.

Harrison actually did live in the West anyway, in the town his father-in-law had founded, North Bend, Ohio. He had built a five-room log cabin there in 1795, after he became engaged to Anna Symmes. By 1840 the log cabin was only a corner of a much-annexed house—but the Baltimore journalist who gibed at "Granny Harrison" didn't know that. His uninformed comment about log cabins and hard cider was thus seized upon gleefully by the Whigs. It was just the fuel they needed to spark their campaign fires.

"Which do you want," was their campaign cry, "a man of the frontier, an Indian fighter living in a log cabin and drinking hard cider—or someone who dabs himself with cologne and sips champagne poured from a silver cooler?"

Log cabins were built as campaign headquarters. Tippecanoe handkerchiefs, log cabin badges, and miniature cider-barrel-shaped lapel pins appeared all across the country. There were grand parades, each one featuring a log cabin on wheels. So many campaign songs were written that people lost count of them.

One of the campaign stunts which certainly pleased the candidate's seven-year-old grandson, Benjamin Harrison, was the rolling from town to town of a huge paper ball. Ten feet in diameter and covered with Whig slogans, it was propelled by ten men shouting: "Keep the ball rolling on to Washington!"

Undoubtedly, Ben and his brothers and sisters delighted in singing the song that the stunt inspired, too:

"It is the ball a-rolling on
For Tippecanoe and Tyler, too!"

When the campaign to make Benjamin Harrison President of the United States began, some politicians thought it would be clever to "get the ball rolling" in the same sort of demonstrations that had worked for Harrison's grandfather. They set up log cabins as campaign headquarters and tried publicizing their candidate as "Young Tippecanoe."

"Little Ben's big enough to wear the hat of his grandfather, Old Tippecanoe!" they cried.

A Democratic cartoonist gleefully lampooned this boast, drawing a little man almost hidden under an outsize beaver hat, and bowed under the weight of it.

The subject of all this was not amused. Proud though he was of his ancestry, Benjamin Harrison did not want to wear any hat but his own.

CHAPTER 2

Thoughtful Ben

BENJAMIN HARRISON had always been encouraged to stand on his own two feet and stride forward unafraid. Fortunately, his upbringing would guide his steps in the right direction.

He was born in his grandfather's house at North Bend, Ohio, on August 20, 1833. His father, John Scott Harrison, had been left in charge of it and the accompanying farm lands while William Henry Harrison was away in Colombia. He had done such a good job that William Henry, on his return from South America, had asked his son to stay on awhile.

When Benjamin was three, John was rewarded by a deed of farm property five miles below North Bend on the Ohio River at its intersection with the Miami. On that land, known as The Point, John had a square brick house erected. There Benjamin grew up.

He had plenty of company. In his own family there were four girls and four boys. Often some of John's nephews also lived with the Harrisons, and there were many neighbor children as well.

None of them received public education. Instead, John had a small log cabin school built between the river and the house and employed private tutors to teach there.

The school was no more luxurious than a public school of the time. The floor was of rough timber, the windows

few and small. At one end was a great fireplace, in cold
weather filled with logs that would burn all day. The
benches were just slabs raised above the floor by sticks fitted
in through auger holes. The benches were backless and so
high that little fellows like Ben could not touch the floor
with their feet. They had to sit for hours with their legs
dangling. Ben was bright and liked to study from the day
he began his ABC's, but he always rejoiced when recess
came and he could run the blood back into his weary legs.

School did not make up the whole of his days. He had to
help with planting and harvesting. He also shared with
his brothers the tasks of carrying wood and water, feeding
the horses, cattle, hogs, and sheep.

There were sports, too. Ben, though smaller than average,
had plenty of spirit and gumption, and he often took the
lead in rough games. The nearby woods and the river attracted him too. He early became an avid angler and an
expert shot, supplying the family table with fish, squirrels,
and ducks too, when they were in season.

Frequently Ben took his grandmother, Mrs. William
Henry Harrison, a pair of ducks or a brace of pigeons. She
had always been one of Ben's favorites, and after her husband's untimely death only a month after his inauguration
as President, Ben made a point of visiting her even more
often. Anna Harrison was always delighted to see Ben and
proud to accept his gifts as evidence of his expertise at manly
sports.

Ben's whole family spent Sundays with the elder Mrs.
Harrison at North Bend. They attended church together
and afterwards returned to her home for dinner. It had
always been General Harrison's custom to offer a blanket
invitation of hospitality to the entire congregation, and
Mrs. Harrison kept up the tradition. There was seldom a
Sunday when places were set for less than fifty people. And

yet, as Ben was to learn before long, Mrs. Harrison was not
overblessed with riches. Everything that appeared on her
table was produced on her farm, unless she had "held over"
something that Ben had contributed. At such times, she
made a point of telling her guests about it. No doubt Ben
was gratified to hear them murmur: "He's a chip off the old .
block," knowing that the "old block" was Old Tippecanoe
himself.

Ben was perfectly happy at The Point, but the time came
when he had learned all that the tutors could teach him.
Since he was only fourteen, his parents did not want him
to go too far away to school. They chose the nearest good
one they could find: Farmer's College, in Cincinnati.

It was not really a college at all, but rather a pre-college.
It did have excellent instructors, and from them Ben got
a good grounding in Latin, Greek, mathematics, and phi-
losophy. He managed to have a good time as well. According to Lew Wallace, the biographer whom Benjamin Harrison himself chose to write the "true story" of his life, Ben
as a boy spent much leisure at "snowballing, town-ball,
bull-pen, shinny and baste," all of which were presumably
games. He also delighted in the library books he found at
Farmer's College, for—again according to Wallace—"he
drank deeply from Dickens, Thackeray, and all the modern classicists; occasionally he read the Cooper stories and
the tales of Washington Irving."

Evidently Ben's mother worried about his having too
good a time, and perhaps about filling his head with too
much romanticism as well. She wrote him mildly admon-
ishing letters, reminding him what he was at school for
and adding that, when he read, he should not forget the
Bible. As an elevating change of pace she recommended
Pilgrim's Progress.

Invariably Elizabeth Harrison closed her letters with the

words "I pray for you daily." From babyhood Ben had known that, every night before she went to bed, his mother spent a few moments on her knees in prayer. Away from her as he was then, he felt warmed by the knowledge that she was interceding for him with the Lord. He equated her influence as almost divine, in his thoughts paraphrasing the forty-sixth Psalm to read: "She is my refuge and strength, a very present help in time of trouble."

Ben said, "I felt as if a rug had been pulled out from under me," when his mother died during his last year at Farmer's College. Her death profoundly affected Ben's thinking. In a letter thanking one of his teachers for a message of condolence, he wrote: "How such events should impress us with the necessity of making our peace with God!"

The impression stayed with him. Soon after he entered Miami University in the fall of 1850, he took the necessary instructions and became a member of the Presbyterian Church. This was not just a gesture on his part, taken because his mother had been a devout Presbyterian. He did realize, however, that she had been a prop for him, and that her strength had come in large measure from her religious convictions. Now he himself needed a faith to live by.

In taking his oath of loyalty to the Presbyterian Church, Benjamin Harrison accepted the Scriptures of the Old and New Testaments as the Word of God and "the only infallible rule of faith and practice." He embraced the belief that he was living in a moral universe where sin carried its own penalty and righteousness its own reward. He was made conscious of the connection of honor, integrity, and every noble virtue with his profession of religion, and from that day forward he carried the knowledge in the foreground of his mind. It was to influence all his subsequent career.

This Christian conscientiousness led him to give far
greater attention to his studies at Miami University than
he had at Farmer's College. A fellow student, Lewis W.
Ross, said of him, "His manner was indicative of much
earnestness of character. He never seemed to regard life
as a joke nor the opportunities for advancement as subjects for sport. . . . He always did his best."

His best, of course, was better in some subjects than in
others. He liked history and political science; indeed, he
took special interest in any study that led him to consider
questions of social or political life.

Ben early exhibited the qualities that produce orators.
He had a good voice and pure diction. On any subject that
aroused him, he spoke easily and well. When he became a
member of the Union Literary Society, he took full advantage of every opportunity to do public speaking and
to take part in debates. The topics chosen were the important religious and political questions of the day, and
the participants were encouraged to speak their opinions
freely. Since the university library contained all important
volumes in those fields, as well as many government papers
and other official reports, Ben found much food for his
mind.

Ben also became one of the first members of the social
fraternity Phi Delta Theta. He was, in fact, the nineteenth
signer of the Greek-letter bond, and all his life he retained
an interest in the fraternity's welfare.

Ben's life in Oxford, Ohio, was not confined wholly to
the campus of Miami University. The town boasted another seat of learning, Oxford Female College. The year
Ben entered Miami, a former teacher of his at Farmer's
College, Dr. John W. Scott, became president of the girls'
institution. His daughter, Carrie, was a student there.

Ben had known Carrie in Cincinnati, and they had enjoyed an uncomplicated friendship there. Now, though,

they were both older—he was seventeen, she sixteen—when they met again in Oxford. It wasn't long before they realized that they were truly happy only when they were together. Though they could not hope to marry for several years, they became engaged.

The engagement had the effect of making Ben study harder than ever. He had decided that he would be a lawyer, and he wanted to get through with formal study and take up the profession as soon as possible.

In those days, a course of study did not have to cover a certain number of years. It could be completed as slowly or as rapidly as an individual student qualified. Ben was ready to be graduated in less than two years, in June of 1852. He stood fourth in a class of sixteen and was asked to give an oration.

He chose as his subject "The Poor of England." It was a topic he had meant to discuss in the Literary Society, but the right time for it had never come. He delighted in the chance to make his views known to a captive audience now.

As with everything he undertook, Ben had lavished a great deal of time and thought on his subject. He had tried to find out the cause that led to the pauperism of so large a section of England's population. He concluded that it was the direct result of her Poor Laws. He thought they destroyed a man's incentive to work, because he would have "the ever-present consciousness that, however great his improvidence and vice, he cannot be brought to ultimate want." In other words, Ben felt it was demoralizing to a man's character to know he'd be taken care of even if he didn't lift a finger to help himself. The Poor Laws took away honest pride of self and replaced it with selfishness. This, Ben's Presbyterian conscience could not approve. In his speech he said, "Heaven and hell are . . . states of mind and character. They have their commencement in the here and now. An utterly selfish man can find no happiness in heaven because he carries hell in his heart." This belief, uttered by Benjamin Harrison at age nineteen, is worth noting well, because it was a belief he was to hold all his life.

After commencement Ben went home to The Point with the members of his family who had come to see him graduated. Taking leave of Carrie was hard, but necessary. She still had another year of school to finish. He had to prove to her father that he was a man and that he was capable of making a livelihood.

Fortunately, Ben's father was prepared to treat him like a man. John Harrison discussed financial affairs with his son for the first time. And Ben was appalled to learn that family affairs were in a sad state. Over the years, his father had loaned money here, signed notes for friends there, and seldom taken proper surety for himself. When the notes came due and the friends had no money to pay, Mr. Harrison mortgaged pieces of his land to meet the payments. Eventually came judgments and foreclosures, and by such means five hundred acres of Harrison farmland had dwindled to just a few.

Ben realized at once how great a sacrifice it must have been for his father to keep him in college. He was determined that he would never again add to the family financial burden.

John Harrison knew, of course, that his son's heart was set on being a lawyer, and indeed he had anticipated enrolling Ben in the law department of Cincinnati College. But when he saw that Ben was adamant about not accepting another penny, he acknowledged the decision with good grace.

The alternative to formal study was apprenticeship in a law office. Ben allowed his father to pull the necessary strings to get him accepted in the notable Cincinnati firm of Storer and Gwynne. Board and lodging, he knew, would cost him nothing. He could live with his married sister, Betsey Eaton, and her doctor husband, who had long ago invited him.

Bellamy Storer, the senior partner of the firm where Ben was privileged to apprentice, had been a Whig congressman for two years. It was therefore quite natural that politics should be often the subject of discussion between him and his associates. This was particularly true in 1852, a presidential campaign year.

Ben had felt himself a Whig from boyhood—ever since the campaign that had culminated in his grandfather's election to the Presidency. But the issues in the campaign of 1852 were different from those of previous campaigns. In 1840, in fact, the Whigs had not even adopted a platform. Still more of a coalition (made up of people who were dissatisfied with other parties) than an organized party, they let William Henry Harrison run for office on the sole ground that Van Buren didn't deserve to be President.

The Democrats had taken a bit more of a stand. They had declared themselves (1) *for* "strict constructionist doctrine," denying that the framers of the Constitution had any other intentions than were expressed in the language they used and allowing for no "interpretation" of it, and (2) *for* the principles of the Declaration of Independence and *against* congressional interference with slavery. This last point is important because it was the *first formal introduction of the slavery question into the platform of a major political party.*

In 1844, when Henry Clay was the Whig candidate opposing Democrat James K. Polk, the Whigs' platform was hardly more than a general statement of party principles. They advocated a single term for the President, a protective tariff, and "internal improvements" (which they left unspecified). They made no mention of the burning issues of the day: the reoccupation of Oregon Territory (of which England was claiming a part) and the annexation of Texas (a separate Republic).

The Democrats, on the other hand, came out strongly in favor of both, thus appealing to all the northerners who wanted Oregon and the southerners who wanted Texas because it would be a slave state. Polk easily won over Clay in that election.

By 1848 the Oregon and Texas questions had been settled. Now the issue was slavery itself. The Democrats, nominating General Lewis Cass, denied the power of Congress to interfere with slavery in the states and criticized all efforts to bring the slavery question before Congress. The Whigs, once again, took no firm stand. Instead, their platform was scarcely more than a recital of their candidate's, General Zachary Taylor's, military character and reputation.

In this campaign, however, there was a third party, made up (as the Whigs had been originally) of disgruntled voters. Calling themselves the Free Soil Party, they adopted as their slogan "Free soil, free speech, free labor, and free men." They pledged themselves to a national platform of freedom, in opposition to the sectional platform of slavery. They failed to carry a single state in the election, but by depriving Cass of enough electoral votes they gave the election to Taylor.

Now in 1852 the mutterings of the storm to come were heard in the South, and no party could ignore them. The candidates were: for the Free Soilers, John P. Hale; for the Whigs, General Winfield Scott; and for the Democrats, Franklin Pierce. The Whigs and the Democrats came out with similar platforms. They accepted in its entirety the Compromise of 1850 and condemned further agitation on the slavery question.

That compromise had called forth the greatest debate

in senatorial history—a free-for-all, really, involving a dozen
senators speaking for and against the Compromise. Briefly,
what happened is this. On January 29, Henry Clay introduced a series of resolutions as a design for settling differences between North and South. They provided for (1)
admission of California as a free state, (2) the organization
of Utah and New Mexico Territories without restriction
on slavery, (3) adjustment of the Texas–New Mexico
border, (4) assumption of the debt contracted by Texas
before its annexation, (5) abolition of the slave trade in the
District of Columbia, and (6) a more effectual law for the
return of fugitive slaves.

Senators immediately took sides. Most notably, the fiery
John C. Calhoun of South Carolina spoke against it, seconded by Jefferson Davis of Mississippi; Daniel Webster of
Massachusetts spoke for it, seconded by Stephen A. Douglas
of Illinois.

Clay's resolutions were finally referred to a Committee
of Fifteen, who did little more than combine the six resolutions into two bills. Finally Congress passed the Compromise—only to have President Taylor object. However,
Taylor died in July, 1850, and brought his Vice-president,
Millard Fillmore, to the highest office in the land. Fillmore favored what was then called "Clay's Compromise,"
and so the bill passed.

As seems obvious from the fact that both Whigs and
Democrats still thought it necessary in 1852 to "approve"
it, the Compromise of 1850 was not universally accepted.
The Free Soil Party, in fact, condemned it, swearing they
would see the bill repealed. The famous philosopher and
poet Ralph Waldo Emerson wrote explosively: "This filthy
enactment was made in the nineteenth century by people
who can read and write. I will not obey it, by God!" He
was referring specifically to the section about fugitive slaves,

because he "couldn't stomach the idea of hunting runaways in the streets and countrysides."

The contest, then, was really not between political parties as people understood them. It was between men who believed in the Union at any price and men who would rather secede from the Union than give up their "rights."

On the surface, it would seem that since the platforms of the two major parties were so similar, there was no specific reason to vote for Scott instead of Pierce, or vice versa. Undercurrents, however, were present. Franklin Pierce was a New Englander who was known to be sympathetic to the South. Winfield Scott, on the other hand, was suspected of having strong anti-slavery sentiments and was thus personally closer to the standard-bearer of the Free Soil Party.

The result was an overwhelming victory for the Democrats and an all but killing defeat for both the Whigs and the Free Soilers.

Ben now found himself forced to re-examine his own stand. What were his beliefs? He believed slavery was morally wrong, yet he acknowledged that men south of the parallel of 36° 30′ (the Missouri border) had a legal right to hold slaves. In line with that thinking, he could not approve the *extension* of slavery anywhere above that parallel. Further, he believed that strict American principles should always be at the front as issues. Everything should be considered as to what was good for America as a nation.

After some soul-searching, Ben came up with the conclusion that *of all existing parties* the Whig Party still came closest to standing for what he believed. The interesting thing is that, when not yet old enough to vote, Ben was already thinking that in none of the existing parties could he feel completely comfortable.

CHAPTER 3

In Practice for Himself

THROUGHOUT THE WINTER and spring of 1852–53, Ben, as law apprentice, kept his nose pretty close to the grindstone. He was given many legal papers to copy, and he tried to learn from them as he wielded his pen. Both Mr. Storer and Mr. Gwynne coached him in legal practices and techniques, too, and assigned him helpful books to study.

Ben's friends tried to coax him to leaven his days of toil with the yeast of an occasional "night on the town." Cincinnati was a growing metropolis and had much to offer of a cultural nature—concerts, lectures, art exhibits—as well as the ever changing and exciting bustle of a busy waterfront. Ben, however, wanted only to get his apprenticeship over with so he could start in practice for himself.

Meanwhile, the main thing that made life worth living was the correspondence he kept up with Carrie, who was finishing her studies in the Oxford Female College.

When Ben felt he had to "get away from Cincinnati or burst," he went home to The Point. There one June day his father told him that their Whig neighbors wanted him, John Harrison, to represent Hamilton County in the United States Congress. Ben was pleased that his father was held in such esteem and urged him to accept.

His father said that he wanted to, but that he hesitated because of the necessity of leaving Ben's motherless younger brothers and sisters virtually alone at The Point. To be sure, their grandmother, Mrs. William Henry Harrison, was living there now, but she was quite old.

Ben's quick mind jumped to the perfect solution for the dilemma. He and Carrie could marry and live at The Point. He could commute to Cincinnati daily—lots of people did —until his apprenticeship was finished. Then—well, what he would do then was in the lap of the gods.

So it was decided and so it happened. On October 20, 1853, Carrie and Ben were married. On December 6, John Harrison left to take up his duties in the national House of Representatives.

The elder Harrison was uncertain how influential he could be in Congress, since as a Whig member he would be decidedly in the minority there. Besides, thanks to the Compromise of 1850, the ship of state seemed to be sailing on smooth waters. He was not the kind of man who would deliberately create waves. Still, he had the uneasy feeling that what was taken for calm was really the deceptively peaceful eye of a hurricane.

He was uneasy, too, he admitted, as to how President Pierce would stand if a sectional storm should arise. Though a New Englander, Pierce, while yet in Congress, had shown his dislike for "the disruptive affects of abolitionist agitation."

Carrie and Ben settled down happily at The Point. All who lived there were captivated by the charming new lady of the house, for she seemed to know instinctively how to please each one. They told her over and over that they hoped she'd never go away. Wisely, she made no promises.

In March, 1854, lawyers Storer and Gwynne agreed that Ben was ready to apply to the Ohio bar for permission to practice in the state. He did so and, with such backing, had no trouble in qualifying.

This first important milestone in Ben's career had an

almost immediate effect on the still underage young man. Now he wanted to take Carrie and go away someplace where he could be his own man, where he would have to start from scratch to make a name for himself.

Carrie, in sympathy with Ben's desires, was ready to go wherever he wished. First, though, there were some important matters to be decided. For one, where did Ben want to settle? For another, how would they live until Ben started to earn something? And third, was John Harrison counting on their staying at The Point all the time he was in Washington?

Ben wrote to his father for the answer to the third question, at the same time explaining what he wanted to do and why. Mr. Harrison replied that of course Ben should do as he thought best. There would be no problem at The Point, because Ben's older brother Irwin was returning. As for money to live on, he—John Harrison—had a regular income from the Congress now. He would give them a going-away present of $500.

Ben and Carrie, happy that two birds had been killed with one stone, then set about to answer the remaining question: Where should they go? To some big city other than Cincinnati, certainly, but which? Soon they narrowed the possibilities to two: Chicago and Indianapolis.

Chicago was ruled out when Ben received a letter from a disillusioned lawyer friend who had moved there, so that left Indianapolis. There Ben did have a connection of sorts—a foster sister of John Harrison and her husband, William Sheets. Sheets was a successful businessman in Indianapolis, a pioneer in the manufacture of paper.

Ben went to Indianapolis to inspect the city personally. The Sheets were not at home, but all whom Ben met were most cordial to him. He returned to The Point very favorably impressed with the city and the challenge it offered an energetic, serious-minded young man.

Friends tried to dissuade Ben from leaving Cincinnati, where he had contacts who could easily channel business his way. He, however, believed that a man should make his way on merit alone. And he was a man now, no matter how boyish he looked.

He did look younger than his almost twenty-one years. He was short—barely five-feet-six—and had small hands and feet. He was blond and had a clear pink-and-white complexion. Unquestionably, his youthful appearance distressed him, for he was trying hard to grow a beard. He hoped that by the time he moved to Indianapolis he would have more than blond fuzz to show for his efforts.

The move was hastened by an unexpected happening. An aunt, a Mrs. Findlay, died and left Ben a parcel of real estate in Cincinnati. He sold it for $800, which, together with the $500 promised him by his father, he thought would keep him and Carrie comfortably while he was getting a foothold in Indianapolis legal circles.

In the 1850's, what would today seem a short move was long and tiring. The young couple had to go the fourteen miles from North Bend, Ohio, to Lawrenceburg, Indiana, by wagon, carrying with them boxes of provisions, some bedding, and a few other necessities for housekeeping. In Lawrenceburg they got a train on the recently completed Indianapolis and Cincinnati Railroad. But the train was less comfortable even than the spring wagon, for the roadbed was rough and the seats hard and unyielding. Undoubtedly, Ben and Carrie were very glad when the four-and-a-half hour ride was over and they were at last in Indianapolis.

Indianapolis, located within five miles of the geographical center of the state, was ideally situated to be the capital of Indiana. Laid out in 1820 on the west fork of the White River, the original town plot had been one mile square. At the time of its incorporation in 1821 it had had less than a thousand inhabitants. But it had grown rapidly. By 1847 it had more than 8,000 citizens, and now in 1854 double that figure. According to the Indianapolis Directory of 1857: "From 1847 to 1850, several saw and grist mills, two foundries, steam engine and machine shops, a peg-and-last factory, a planing mill, several slaughter houses . . . were built and put into operation." And the number and variety of businesses and factories were increasing daily.

Ben's "courtesy cousin," William Sheets, met the Harrisons at the train and took them home with him to stay until they could find suitable quarters. He made their looking easier by showing them around the city himself. He reminded Ben how great a part his grandfather, William Henry Harrison, had played in securing the area for settlement. Ben could surely recall many times when William Henry had talked of the territory over which he had been governor. Although the Indians had had no village on the present location of Indianapolis, they had often camped along the riverbank while hunting and fishing. Ben remembered that then deer, turkeys, and pigeons had been plentiful, and the river so full of fish, one had only to drop in a line to ensure oneself a meal. He wondered if it still was, and whether he'd have a chance to find out.

Pleasant as it was being pampered guests in the Sheets' household, Ben and Carrie wanted nothing so much as to have a place all their own. Accordingly, Ben rented the ground floor of a two-story flat on Pennsylvania Avenue, even though the $7 a week was more than he could comfortably afford.

Once settled, Ben set about making his availability for legal counseling known. However, as his Cincinnati friends had warned, business was hard to come by for an unknown. Besides, Ben's appearance would not automatically attract clients to him. How could he prove he was able in spite of his immature looks?

Ben's first year in Indianapolis could not be called successful. To keep busy, he spent many hours in abstract offices, hunting up titles, getting paid only a pittance for his labor. Being optimistic, he was not discouraged, but he was hard up for money. The stake he had been sure would last him and Carrie until he was established was fast disappearing. Carrie was pregnant and required medicines and the attention of a doctor. Also, in order to conserve her strength, she needed someone to help her with the household tasks.

Carrie's parents suggested that perhaps it would be wise if Carrie returned to live with them until the baby was born. Though the young couple did not wish to be separated, it did appear to be the sensible thing to do. So Carrie went to Oxford, and Ben took lodgings alone.

In his lonesomeness without Carrie, Ben did sometimes seek the company of William Sheets. Sheets, who had been in Indiana politics some years before, still knew some politicians. He introduced Ben to John H. Rea, then Clerk of the United States District Court.

It was a lucky introduction. Rea was delighted to know that another Harrison was interesting himself in Indiana, and he saw that Ben met people who might do him some good.

Ben had no wish to ride on the coattails of his grandfather, but he could not in conscience turn down Rea's offer. Thanks to it, he soon received an appointment as crier of the federal court, at a salary of $2.50 a day, during term time.

The regular income, though not large, gave a lift to his spirits, and he felt better able to be patient until business should come his way. While waiting, he set about mastering the Indiana statutes and the code of practice in that state. He wanted to be thoroughly prepared when his first chance at trial work should arise.

It was Major Jonathan W. Gordon, the prosecuting

attorney for Marion County, who gave him that chance. Major Gordon had noticed Ben's industry and attention to all that went on around the court. And at this particular time the case before it was the so-called Point Lookout burglary.

The trial was to come up for hearing in the afternoon. Major Gordon was afraid it would be continued into the night—and he wanted to attend a lecture by the educator Horace Mann, Free Soil candidate for the Presidency in 1852 and now president of Antioch College. So Major Gordon asked Ben if he'd assist him with the case and be prepared to make the concluding appeal to the jury if the trial should last into the evening.

The attorney for the defense was a well-known figure, an ex-governor of Indiana, David Wallace. More than that, his was a name familiar to Ben since childhood. Mr. Wallace had been a friend of William Henry Harrison—so good a friend that, when Harrison was territorial governor, he had appointed Wallace's son to the West Point cadetship coveted by his own son, John. Governor Wallace was, moreover, one of the most brilliant lawyers in the state of Indiana.

The possibility of meeting such competition in his first trial might have made any young lawyer shake in his shoes. Ben did have qualms, but he never considered turning down Major Gordon's offer. He spent the afternoon making detailed notes about every shred of testimony.

The trial, as Major Gordon had anticipated, was continued to the evening, and at supper he gave Ben the responsibility of summing up the state's case.

Ben had never been in the old courthouse at night before, and he thought the place looked forbidding. As he later described it to his official biographer, Lew Wallace, in 1888: "On the fixed desk before the judge there were two dim tallow candles lighted. . . . On the pillars in the center of the room, and here and there upon the walls, were old-fashioned tin sconces, casting a glow red and murky with smoke." In the shadows a crowd waited, ready to applaud or deride his maiden effort.

When Ben took his place at his table, he discovered that it too was only dimly lighted. Now he was truly distressed. To be sure of being absolutely correct in his comments, he had planned to read his summation to the jury. Would he be able to see the paper?

The moment he rose to his feet, he knew he would not. He would have to rely upon his memory.

Fortunately, the natural aptitude for extemporaneous speaking Ben had shown at Miami University, now, after the first hesitant moments, reasserted itself in the court-room. He remembered all the important points he had wanted to make, and he knew he was explaining them in language that was fresh and convincing.

Convincing it was. Even Governor Wallace, who as defense attorney had the closing speech, was honest enough to say so. The verdict was obvious, but the jury had to make a show of retiring to consider it. The panel stayed out only long enough for a formal polling of votes. The decision— for the prosecution: guilty as charged.

Benjamin Harrison's first trial was hailed as a triumph. News of it spread quickly, and soon a trickle of clients began flowing his way. Ben wrote Carrie happily, assuring her that as soon as the baby was born they would get a house and live together as a family in Indianapolis.

Ben had hoped the birth would coincide with his own twenty-first birthday (August 20, 1854), but the baby Russell was born eight days earlier, on August 12. Ben's hope for an immediate reunion in Indianapolis faded, too, because he was advised by a physician friend that late summer and early fall were "unhealthy and damp" in that city. He wrote Carrie to tell her so, and they agreed that she should go instead to The Point, where the country air was fresh and invigorating.

When Carrie and the baby finally arrived, on October 9, Ben rented a three-room house on Vermont Street. It was tiny, yet it was all they required. Carrie could do most of the work herself. What she could not manage, Ben could. He sawed wood for her, filled water buckets, even cared for the baby now and then. He assured her it was all easy work, compared to the chores he had done as a child around The Point.

For a while they were in a tight financial squeeze, because they had agreed that Ben should have his own tiny office. As long as they were all well, it didn't matter. But by Christmas of that year, 1854, both Carrie and the baby were sick. Ben felt he had to let them go back to Ohio again, to divide their time between The Point and Oxford. By New Year's Day, 1855, the bottom had dropped out of Ben's finances, too.

His plight was not of his making. All of Indiana was suffering from a business depression; exactly why, no one seemed to know. Banks were discounting their notes. Railroads suspended operations. Traders' and manufacturers' business dropped almost to nothing. Only lawyers who were well established had any clients at all.

As happens so often in times of unrest, men blamed the status quo for their troubles. In regard to politics, it meant agitation for a new party that would change things for the better. Such was the thought behind the organization of the Republican Party in 1854, and also of the short-lived People's Party.

It was the latter that had immediate significance for Ben. William Wallace—a successful lawyer, son of the ex-governor whom Ben had opposed in his first trial—had joined the People's Party, and he planned to be loyal to it. To him that meant running for office on the People's ticket. He needed someone to mind his law office. Having heard good things from his father about "young Harrison," in March, 1855, he asked Ben to become his law partner, beginning at once.

Ben took over the clients and the practice, leaving Wallace free to stump Marion County in the hope of gaining the county clerkship.

CHAPTER 4

First Step into Politics

WALLACE'S CANVASS took him from his practice for much of the next two months, but Ben proved himself up to the challenge he had accepted. He not only took care of the firm's old clients but even acquired some new ones. Wallace was more than pleased with his young partner. According to a letter the senior member wrote at the time: "He very soon disclosed his admirable qualities as a lawyer—quick of comprehension, clear, methodical and logical in his analysis and statement of a case. He possessed a natural faculty for getting the exact truth out of a witness, either by direct or cross-examination . . . when the cause demanded it, illustrating the rarest powers of the genuine orator."

Ben was glad to be "blessedly busy," as he wrote Carrie, so long as she was away, because he could bear her absence better. Frequently he found himself working all day and far into the night.

Wallace was defeated at the polls, and so he returned to take up his practice again. Fortunately, his return coincided with that of Carrie and Russell; otherwise the Harrison family life would have suffered.

Part of life for both Ben and Carrie since childhood had been daily prayer and Bible reading. Now, as a couple, they became members of the First Presbyterian Church of Indianapolis and entered into its program with dedication. Ben became a teacher in the Sabbath School and also

worked with young men in the Y.M.C.A. The church provided them, too, with a full social life.

Another part of life for Ben had naturally been politics,
ever since the exciting campaign of 1840 which had led to
his grandfather's election to the Presidency. With his father
now a member of the Congress, Ben was kept up-to-date on
what was going on in Washington and, indeed, in the
nation.

The most exciting controversy of 1854 had concerned the
Kansas-Nebraska Bill, introduced in the Senate on January
23 by Democrat Stephen A. Douglas of Illinois. Douglas had
proposed the admission of the territories of Kansas and
Nebraska *with or without slavery*. The bill, if passed, would
virtually repeal the Missouri Compromise of 1820, which
prohibited slavery north of the parallel of 36° 30′, and
would formally establish the doctrine of congressional nonintervention in the territories.

Douglas's proposal at once aroused a storm of protest.
John Harrison was among the congressmen to object. As he
wrote Ben, he was troubled about the breaking of a solemn
compact made when Missouri was admitted to the Union.
He was afraid Douglas's action was designed to appease the
South, so that his way might be smoothed there for a slide
into the Presidency. However, conservative Whig that
Harrison was, he was not willing to do anything more
drastic about the bill than vote against it.

A number of disillusioned Democrats, led by Charles
Sumner and Salmon P. Chase, were not as reluctant as Whig
Harrison. They denounced the bill as a gross violation of a
sacred pledge. They charged further that the measure was
the work of a slaveholder conspiracy. And in January, they
published an Appeal incorporating those charges.

Despite all the opposition, the Kansas-Nebraska Act was
passed by Congress in May, 1854. Its passage caused realign-

ment of political forces in the North and West. The immediate impact was felt in the northwest, where men of all parties united on a platform opposing the extension of slavery. A meeting of dissatisfied Whigs, Free Soilers, and antislavery Democrats recommended the organization of a new party on this single principle and suggested the name Republican. Among its leaders were two who had signed the published Appeal of the Independent Democrats the previous January: Charles Sumner and Salmon P. Chase.

Whiggery was now all but dead, and even John Harrison felt compelled to resort to new political alliance. He could not approve what he called the "incendiary" ideas held by the Republicans. Neither could he go along with the state's rights ideas of the Democrats. He therefore aligned himself with the American, or Know-Nothing, Party, which had been founded in 1852 on the convenient premise that foreign groups were responsible for all the disorders of the country. Now it was really a compromise party, standing firmly by the Compromise of 1850 as the salvation of the nation.

Ben had always shared his father's admiration for the party of William Henry Harrison. Now in 1854, when he was finally old enough to vote, that party was no more. He, like his father, would have to choose another affiliation.

He did not, however, share his father's views about the Republicans. His partner, William Wallace, was active in the Republican Party, now that it had incorporated the People's Party of which he had been a member. And certainly Wallace's ideas were *not* incendiary. In fact, the only point on which he and Ben seemed to have any difference of opinion was on the slavery issue. Although Ben would never keep slaves himself, he did believe that the institution of slavery was entitled to such protection as the Constitution offered.

Then, in October, 1854, while on a business trip to
Peoria, Illinois, Ben heard a still only locally known lawyer, Abraham Lincoln, speak.

Lincoln started out condemning the Kansas-Nebraska
Act. He asserted that under it the slavery agitation had
"not only not ceased but been constantly augmented." He
went on to acknowledge the constitutional rights of the
southerners, but he maintained that, nevertheless, slavery
was morally wrong. He advocated, as a solution, "gradual
emancipation." **1521621**

Ben realized instantly that here was a man with whom he
could agree wholeheartedly, and he went home to Indianapolis singing Lincoln's praises.

The opening of Kansas to settlement in 1855 put Douglas's "popular sovereignty" formula—the power of the people to admit or exclude slavery—to a severe test. The nation,
watching in horror, saw proslavery and free state advocates
resort to shooting in their efforts to get control of the territory. Neither force would give in. The result was that by
the end of the year Kansas had two governors and two
legislatures.

By terms of the Kansas-Nebraska Act, Congress had
forfeited the right to intervene in Kansas. President Pierce,
however, evidently felt that the national government should
make some stand on the matter. In a special message to
Congress on January 24, 1856, he recognized the proslavery
legislature, using as his sole argument the fact that it had
been the first formally elected. He further warned that the
civil war in that state must cease.

Actual civil war, wide scale, broke out in Kansas in the
spring of 1856. On May 21, the free state capital of Law-
rence was taken and sacked, "border ruffians" from neigh-
boring Missouri joining Kansas proslavery men in burning
down the Free State Hotel, pillaging many homes, and

destroying the offices and presses of *The Herald of Freedom* and *The Kansas Free State.*

John Brown, an abolitionist, sought revenge. He led an attack on a proslavery settlement near Pottawatomie Creek and murdered five settlers. Free State men denied any responsibility for this, but it raised feelings to a murderous pitch, and soon guerilla warfare was raging throughout the territory.

Congress had only one recourse during all this. It could refuse to seat any delegate from the territory of Kansas until the true feeling of the people there was known. John Harrison, however, could privately say anything he wished. With unusual fury, he condemned all people who believed that the "furtherance of Christ's kingdom upon the earth can only be advanced by warfare upon the slaveholder."

Ben did not second his father's sentiments. The people to whom John Harrison referred were the fifteen or so Republican representatives in the lower house, in particular Nathaniel P. Banks, recently elected Speaker, and Ben had just decided to throw in his lot with Banks' party.

That year, 1856, was a presidential election year, and Republicans sought to make "Bleeding Kansas" the chief campaign issue. Their opening gun was a speech made by Senator Charles Sumner that later became known by the title "The Crime Against Kansas." He denounced the "slave oligarchy" (the persons ruling the slave states) so bitterly that his attack was taken personally by several southern senators. The nephew of one, himself a member of the House of Representatives, was so incensed that he brutally beat Sumner with a cane. The injuries to Sumner kept him away from the Senate until December, 1859. The crazy attack was condemned by Republicans as "one more instance of how far slaveholders would go."

In June, 1856, the first Republican National Convention

was held in Philadelphia. Colonel John C. Fremont—
explorer, politician, and soldier—was nominated for the
Presidency. His opponents were the American (Know-
Nothing) Party's Millard Fillmore and the Democrat's
James Buchanan. Buchanan had finally been chosen on the
seventeenth ballot, after the incumbent President Pierce
and the hopeful Stephen Douglas had both been rejected
because of their close association with the Kansas issue.

Benjamin Harrison approved of the platform adopted by
the Republican Party: the right of Congress to control
slavery in the territories; the building of a railroad to the
Pacific; and the admission of Kansas as a free state. He
might not have campaigned actively for it, however, but
the choice was taken out of his hands.

The story of how this came about has often been told.
Ben was peacefully at work in his second-story office when
he heard a great stamping of feet up the staircase. Then an
excited group of his fellow citizens burst in. The leader
took him by the arm, saying they needed a ratification
speech for the Republican platform.

Ben protested. He was a lawyer, he said, not a politician.
But the men would not take no for an answer. They lifted
him to their shoulders and carried him to where a crowd was
waiting. Because he was so short, they set him on a good-
sized box, where he could be seen by the throng. Then,
without warning, the leader introduced him as "young
Tippecanoe."

This Benjamin Harrison would not allow to pass un-
challenged.

"I want it understood," he said, "that I do not wish to be
acclaimed as the grandson of anybody. I think every man
should stand on his own merits."

Once having been forced to take the stump, however, he
continued to campaign for a Republican victory in country,

state, and county. He was too late to speak for city candidates, for their election had been lost in May.

James Buchanan, the Democratic candidate, won over Fremont by half a million popular votes; Fremont won over Fillmore by about the same margin. Ben was not mean enough to rub in that fact to his father, for John Harrison had lost his congressional seat in the election.

Ben did rejoice, however, when a special election was held in Indianapolis two weeks later to fill vacancies in the offices of mayor and city clerk. Republicans were elected to both positions.

The excitement engendered by that victory made Ben decide to enter the political arena himself. He accepted the challenge to run for the office of city attorney in the May, 1857, election.

This was regarded by his father as "political conduct unbecoming to a Harrison." Quite aside from party affiliation, the office would bring him no esteem, his father argued. He would be just a "political hack."

Ben, however, had chosen what he thought was the right first step for himself. The duties he would have to assume, if he was elected, were already familiar to him from the time when he had been called to act as assistant prosecuting attorney. They would not be so arduous that he could not continue his legal practice. This was an important thing to consider when a man had a growing family.

Ben was victorious, and his father was man enough to be happy for him. John Harrison wrote him a letter of congratulation, reopening the door for the frequent correspondence between father and son that had dwindled recently due to their political differences.

Those differences did not cease, but now that John had retired from the heat of active politics, he was able to render less impassioned and more reasoned opinions than before. Ben was grateful for this, because he himself was still very unseasoned in the arena and welcomed experienced advice from someone he could trust.

One of Ben's friends at Miami University, Oliver P. Morton, was the leader of the Republican Party in Indiana. He had been defeated in his bid for the governorship of the state in 1856, when Buchanan had carried the Democrats along to victory everywhere, but only by a narrow margin. The Republicans had then swept the Democrats from office in the city elections of 1857, and Morton had predicted a similar sweep of the nation in 1860. Naturally, he hoped to be the state standard-bearer then and he wanted all the big-name support he could get.

Benjamin Harrison had such a name, by virtue of his family connections. Insistent though he was that he did not want to be typed as "the grandson of Old Tippecanoe," the fact made for good publicity.

In his position as city attorney, Ben was doing his usual thoroughgoing job, and this fact too was carefully noted by local Republican leaders. By January, 1858, they were wondering if he would be willing to run for the state legislature.

He was wondering, too. Carrie was expecting a second child in April, so he knew he would not want to go far afield campaigning. He considered too, if he were elected, what would happen to his private practice. Even though the legislature sat right there in Indianapolis, would his clients fear he would slight their business for the state's? And, if he wanted to become known in *national* politics, would this kind of local position be a step forward or sideways?

Before he had to say yes or no definitely, Ben was offered the unelective post of secretary to the State Republican Central Committee. At once Ben decided to turn down the chance to run for the legislature and accept the secretary-

ship. It would teach him about party workings at every
level, as he could learn them no other way. More, it definitely would help him if he later decided he wanted to go
somewhere in politics. It would give him statewide ac-
quaintance with everybody of any importance in the party.

John Harrison criticized this move even more acidly
than he had Ben's acceptance of the city attorneyship.
Didn't Ben know any better than to tie himself so firmly to
the Republican Party? Its fortunes were falling, said John,
not rising. Couldn't Ben see the handwriting on the wall?
Stephen Douglas was going to be the man to reckon with in
the political future!

Nevertheless, for twenty-five-year-old Benjamin Harrison
the die was cast. For better or worse, he *was* tied firmly to
the Republican Party.

CHAPTER 5

The Young Campaigner

JOHN HARRISON's prediction that Douglas was going to be *the* man to reckon with was wrong only in the choice of grammatical article. Douglas was one of two men to reckon with. The other was Abraham Lincoln. On June 17, 1858, Lincoln had accepted the challenge to run against Douglas for the United States Senate.

On that day, at the Republican state convention meeting in Springfield, Illinois, Lincoln had made what has since become known as the "House Divided" speech. In it he had reaffirmed the stand taken when Ben had heard him in Peoria: that under the Kansas-Nebraska Act the slavery agitation had "not only not ceased but been constantly augmented." He had added that, in his opinion, slavery agitation would not cease "until a crisis shall have been reached and passed."

Then he had gone on to say the words still memorized by schoolchildren today: " 'A house divided against itself cannot stand.' I believe this government cannot endure half slave and half free. I do not expect the Union to be dissolved; I do not expect the house to fall; but I do expect it will cease to be divided. It will become all one thing, or all the other."

On July 24, Lincoln had challenged Douglas to a series of debates, and Douglas had accepted. Seven debates were subsequently held, covering the slavery controversy and its impact on politics, law, and government.

These debates illuminated the sharp difference between Lincoln and Douglas. Lincoln was unequivocal in his insistence that slavery was "a moral, a social, and a political wrong." Douglas took the stand that the "rights and wrongs of slavery are nobody's business outside the slave states." Douglas further said: "If each state will only agree to mind its own business, and let its neighbors alone . . . this republic can exist forever divided into free and slave states." This, of course, was the antithesis of Lincoln's "A house divided cannot stand."

Lincoln lost the senatorial election, but he was not destined to step back into the shadows of obscurity. In his debates with Douglas he had manifested qualities of greatness. Newspapers had carried full reports of them, and citizens all across the nation could judge for themselves the merits of the arguments and the plans for meeting the impending crisis. Unquestionably, Lincoln had displayed his genius as an orator and his exceptional knowledge of American history and government. Yet, woven all through the fabric of his Republican rhetoric was a thread of homespun wisdom. He was truly a man of the people, with a faith in them that was as staunch as any Democrat's.

Benjamin Harrison, in his position as state secretary, was privileged to know the grass roots thinking of the Republican leaders of Indiana. They believed that if the Republican Party was to win the White House in 1860, it had to choose a man such as Lincoln, who would have wide appeal to voters. They were beginning to think of dropping William A. Seward, who expected to be the candidate. Seward had been a powerful figure in politics since 1838, when he had first become governor of New York. As a senator from that state, he had taken part in the debate concerning the

Compromise of 1850. He had opposed it, saying that "all legislative compromises are radically wrong and essentially vicious." He had appealed to a higher law justifying refusal of constitutional protection to slavery.

Now, ten years later, Seward had taken a radical stand. He had gone much further than Lincoln, who, for all his "house divided" talk, did acknowledge the constitutional right of the southerners to be slaveholders. Seward had declared that an "irrepressible conflict" was coming, that only by war would it be decided whether the nation should be all slave or all free.

What Indiana thought would have a great deal of importance to the strategy-managers in Washington. Indiana was one of two states (the other being Pennsylvania) that both the Republicans and the Democrats considered indispensable to national success, because it controlled a good many electoral votes.

This was heady knowledge for an eager young politician like Benjamin Harrison. Since he knew all eyes would be on Indiana, he decided to try for nomination on the Republican ticket as Supreme Court reporter for the state.

It would not be an easy nomination to secure. The post was not only dignified but carried a good salary, and there would be other eager aspirants for it. Perhaps Ben wanted to try for it for all these reasons. Either he had what it took to win over others, or he didn't. As for the extra money, there is no doubt it would be very welcome too. His family had outgrown the little house he had been renting when the second baby, Mamie (really, Mary), had been added to their number, so he had negotiated to buy a home. He was finding the money to meet installment payments on it hard to come by.

Both the Democratic and the Republican state conventions were held in Indianapolis. The Democrats came first, assembling early in January. The state ticket they chose was an indication of the way they would jump at the National Convention in June. The Democrats-for-Douglas got all of their men nominated, squashing the Democrats-for-Buchanan. Leading the ticket for the office of governor was Thomas A. Hendricks, a seasoned lawyer who had acquired a personal following while serving as commissioner of the General Land Office.

The Republicans met in February, and Ben won over his fellow candidates in the nomination for the post he coveted. At the head of the ticket was Henry S. Lane, with Ben's friend Oliver P. Morton the nominee for lieutenant-governor.

Ben knew he must soon start to stump the state. He knew also that it was the custom of a candidate to work for the success of his party as well as for himself, since on one might depend the other. He intended to conform to this custom, as long as he could do so honestly. The trouble was he was not at all happy with the platform of the local Republicans. It was even less definite on the matter of slavery extension than the national platform of four years before, but Ben himself felt very strongly on the issue. He couldn't just be vague when talking to the public, when men like Jefferson Davis of Mississippi could introduce such inflammatory resolutions as he had done recently in the Senate.

For Davis had certainly not been indefinite in *his* stand. He had asserted many things, among them that (1) neither Congress nor a territorial legislature was in any way empowered to impair a man's right to hold slaves in the territories, and (2) the federal government should extend all needful protection to slavery there.

These resolutions encouraged political leaders in the lower South to openly threaten secession if the rights of their states were violated. This in turn alarmed men of the upper South, who believed that southern grievances could and should be remedied within the Union.

Ben was already giving prayerful thought to which course he could honorably take, when Abraham Lincoln made his Cooper Union speech. The man from Illinois was still known by name only to most easterners before that appearance in New York City, and a large and distinguished audience had gathered to hear him. The speech he gave was not the extemporaneous sort he had made famous during his debates with Douglas. Each word was carefully weighed. He condemned northern extremism and made an appeal for sectional understanding. He warned of the real and present danger of secession by the southern states but insisted that, in spite of it, no compromise on the slavery extension issue was possible.

When he had finished speaking, the audience knew exactly where Abraham Lincoln stood on the important issue of the time. So too, very shortly, did the rest of the nation, for the speech was printed verbatim in newspapers everywhere. Republican reaction to it was overwhelmingly favorable. Democratic reaction was divided.

Benjamin Harrison, reading it, must have welcomed the chance to take the same ground as this contemporary of his, instead of having to bolster his opinions with reference to speeches by Henry Clay and Daniel Webster. Definite as they had been on the slavery extension issue in 1850, *this* was 1860.

Ben's first chance to make his views public came early in March, when he accompanied an old campaigner, Caleb Blood Smith, to Lebanon, Indiana. Smith was chairman of the Indiana delegation to the National Republican Convention, but he had been a Whig devotee in the days of William Henry Harrison. He told Ben they ought to take a page from the book of those triumphant times to use as fuel for this campaign.

Ben might have retorted that the issues of the present day were inflammatory enough already, but he waited to hear how the eloquent old orator handled them.

Mr. Smith didn't "handle" them at all. He sidled around them, keeping a wary distance. When eventually he did dare to touch them—the matter of Kansas, of secession, of congressional intervention, of slavery—it was as if at the end of a ten foot pole. He spent the lion's share of his time alternately lambasting and making fun of the Democratic candidates.

Judging from the delight expressed by the partisan crowd, Smith's speech had made a hit. The question was, in waging a campaign, was it a candidate's duty to *entertain* or to *inform?*

Ben obviously thought the latter, and he was going to try to perform just that service for the people of Lebanon. That is, he was if they would let him. But it wasn't easy for an unknown actor to follow a star.

The audience, which had risen to give Caleb Smith a standing ovation, had already started to move away when the chairman of the meeting introduced Benjamin Harrison. Perhaps it was the magic last name that made a few of the people hesitate. Perhaps it was the fact that such a short, unremarkable-looking youth actually had the nerve to follow an old charmer like Caleb Smith. Anyway, Ben was given his chance. According to a newspaper account of the occasion: "With almost his first utterance, he caused the crowd to pause . . . another sentence shot out, and more stopped to listen. They began to move back toward the stand, drop into their seats, or lean against trees."

Ben discussed all the issues Smith had scarcely mentioned. He used different words, but the content of his remarks was similar to that which Lincoln had expressed in Peoria, in Springfield, in New York. No compromise with the South was possible. The extension of slave territory must stop, and stop *now*.

Ben's speech was attended to by the people of Lebanon, and by Caleb Smith as well. After it, Smith had a word of caution for Ben. Did Ben remember, he wondered, that what he said would be construed as representative of Republican thinking? Had the party authorized him to take such an unequivocal stand on slavery extension?

The party had not, of course, but Ben was not daunted. He had been brought up to believe that men must have the courage of their convictions. And his father had said only recently, "I like to see a candidate honest and outspoken."

Ben was still too young in the game of politics to realize that it should be played with strategy. An experienced politician knew his audience and tailored his remarks to fit it.

He saw this strategy in action when Lane, the Republican gubernatorial candidate, spoke. In northern Indiana, Lane talked of the need to abolish slavery. But in southern Indiana he talked of "holding the line"—not interfering with slavery in states where it was established, but not permitting it to expand into the territories, either.

But Ben didn't see it as strategy. He saw it as, if not downright dishonesty, at least illogical thinking.

National politics, meanwhile, were getting more and more exciting. Within the Democratic Party, the split was becoming wider and wider. There was no chance that the Southern Democrats and the Democrats-for-Douglas could bridge it before the April National Nominating Convention. This might mean there would be bolters from the ranks when the convention met.

It did. The Southern Democrats insisted on a platform supporting positive protection of slavery in the territories.

The Douglas Democrats reaffirmed the platform of 1856, approving congressional nonintervention. When the Douglas forces carried the day, the delegates of eight southern states withdrew to form a separate convention, at which John C. Breckenridge of Kentucky was nominated for President.

Ben, as secretary to the Indiana Republicans, had perhaps hoped to be invited to go to the May Republican National Convention in Chicago, but he was not. He had to be content to read the Indianapolis *Daily Journal* to find out what was happening. And there was no question that he was delighted when Abraham Lincoln emerged as the nominee.

State politicking had been practically at a standstill during the spring months of feverish interest in the national conventions. After them, however, the Indiana campaigners of both parties set out with renewed zeal. Highlighting the contest now were the debates between men opposing each other for top positions.

Ben was scarcely a top contender, so he was not scheduled to take part in any debate. But he got involved in one quite by accident. He was due to give a speech in Rockville, Indiana, and had planned to simply reiterate the stand he and Lincoln shared. However, when he reached his destination, Ben discovered that through some mix-up the Democratic candidate for governor, Thomas A. Hendricks, was slated to talk at the same time and place as himself. As a way out of the dilemma, the Democrats sponsoring Hendricks had proposed to the Republicans that the two speakers might debate.

This prospect was at first appalling to Ben. "That is a very unfair proposal," he said. "Mr. Hendricks is at the head of the Democratic ticket, while I am at the tail of the Republican ticket!"

His reaction seemed to disturb his friends, and Ben surmised that they felt the Democrats would accuse them (and him) of cowardice. This, of course, was not an accusation he wanted made about him or his party.

"Well, gentlemen," he said, "if we can't get out of this without showing the white feather, you just tell them we will consent."

Hendricks, when told, was not so agreeable. He would not condescend, it seemed, to an actual debate with anyone so insignificant as Ben. He would talk first, for two hours. Then Mr. Harrison, if he still wanted to, could take his turn.

The courtroom in which the meeting took place was filled to the rafters—a common enough happening for Hendricks, no doubt, but a novelty for Ben. When Hendricks appeared, he was greeted by thundering applause. As soon as the room was quiet, he began to speak.

He talked not for two but for four full hours. He managed to hold his audience for the whole time, though toward the end it was obvious that more than a few people were getting restless. When he was finished, however, Hendricks did make one concession to his young opponent.

"I hope you will remain and give your attention to the next speaker," he said.

The people remained, but they greeted Ben with silence. He could not blame them, for they surely must be weary of speeches. He would have to provoke their interest at once, or he would not get it at all.

So he decided to make a debate out of the evening in spite of Mr. Hendricks. He had taken notes as his opponent talked. Now he set up the other's points for all to see—and bowled them over, one by one, like ninepins.

The technique was superb, and the audience was quick to recognize it. Over and over again, yells of enthusiasm greeted Ben's statements. The man who had been chairman of that meeting later commented on it.

"I have heard a great many political debates in my day, but I never heard a man skin an opponent as quickly as Ben Harrison did Tom Hendricks that night."

The story spread rapidly from county to county, and soon the name of Benjamin Harrison was known statewide. If he had needed notoriety in order to win office, he would have had it. But he didn't need it. On October 9, the Indiana voters swept the state Democrats out of office and the Republicans in. In November they did the same for the national ticket.

Not since Old Tippecanoe's victory of 1840 had the Democrats lost Indiana in a national election.

Was it so surprising if Young Tippecanoe, as some people persisted in calling Ben, felt a very personal kind of pride in that knowledge?

CHAPTER 6

The Union Forever

THE REPUBLICAN PARTY had shown that it was the champion of the Union. The third clause of the platform it adopted at the May, 1860, Convention stated the belief "that to the Union of the States this nation owes its unprecedented increase in population, its surprising development of material resources, its rapid augmentation of wealth, its happiness at home and its honor abroad; and we hold in abhorrence all schemes for Disunion, come from whatever source they may."

Months earlier, Abraham Lincoln had gone on record saying: "I believe this government cannot endure permanently half slave and half free . . . it will become all one thing or all the other." At that time, southerners had been in some doubt as to which "one thing" he favored. After his acceptance of the nomination for the Presidency on the Republican ticket, however, they no longer doubted. To them, "Republican" and "northern" were synonymous, and northerners abhorred the institution of slavery.

The dice were cast, therefore, at the moment of Lincoln's election. South Carolina took the first belligerent step. The state's legislature called for a convention, which met and on December 20, 1860, passed an ordinance declaring that "the union now subsisting between South Carolina and the other states . . . is hereby dissolved." Four days later the convention issued a "Declaration of Causes," repeating the old arguments for states' rights and justifying secession on the grounds of (1) the North's long attacks on slavery, (2) the accession to power of a sectional party, and (3) the election of a President whose opinions were hostile to slavery.

Before the January 13, 1861, swearing-in of Benjamin Harrison as reporter of the Supreme Court of the State of Indiana, three more states of the lower South (Mississippi, Florida, and Alabama) had seceded. This fact made Ben's assumption of office, and also Governor Henry Lane's, less exciting to Indianans than such state affairs normally were. The juggling that went on in the following two days, when by obvious prearrangement the brand-new governor was appointed United States senator and Oliver P. Morton stepped up to governor, went almost unnoticed.

Perhaps the newly elected Indiana officers felt sensitive about this lack of attention. Perhaps they only wanted to emphasize Indiana's loyalty to the Union that the lower South had repudiated. Anyway, they had a flagpole installed on top of the State House dome. On January 22, they organized a grand parade through the streets of Indianapolis, with brass bands and the state militia accompanying the bearer of a large American flag.

The parade attracted a huge crowd. Thousands of people watched and cheered as the flag was raised. But it had not even unfurled to the breeze before its pole broke. The red-white-and-blue symbol of the Union crashed from the dome to the roof, and the roar of the crowd turned to a moan of apprehension.

"It was as if a cold hand had touched our hearts," Ben said later.

In the days that followed, the touch became a clutch. The three other states of the lower South (Georgia, Louisiana, and Texas) seceded, too. Four states of the upper South (Virginia, Arkansas, Tennessee, and North Carolina), though not seceding just yet, warned that they would "oppose any attempt of the Federal Government to coerce a state."

President Buchanan, spending his last days in the Presidency, expressed "profound disapproval of the disruption of the Union," but added that the Attorney General had ruled that the federal government was "impotent to prevent secession by force."

Buchanan, of course, was not the man in the hot spot. The man who was, Lincoln, was scheduled to leave for Washington on February 11. He expected to proceed slowly, giving speeches at key cities en route.

His farewell to his neighbors in Springfield was poignant, even prophetic: "I go, not knowing when or whether I ever may return, with a task before me greater than that which rested upon Washington."

Every public statement Lincoln made was meticulously reported. The nation was waiting for some hint of what his plans and policies as President would be. So far he had been noncommittal, so much so that his political opponents were calling him "The Sphinx from Springfield."

Indianapolis was to be one of Lincoln's stops, and the Republicans were busy arranging a proper reception for the President-elect. Even conscientious Benjamin Harrison took time off from his new duties and his legal work to help. He was eager to shake the hand of the man he had admired for so long.

Hours before the special train was due, hundreds of people had collected at the bunting-hung railroad station. Many thousands more were strung out all along the parade route to the Bates House, the hotel where Lincoln was to stay. At precisely five o'clock, the President-elect arrived. He was greeted by a salvo of thirty-four guns, followed by the almost equally deafening roar of welcome from the

crowd. Ben, standing close enough to touch the new national leader, was struck by the quiet, humble bearing of the
man. Here was no firebrand, in spite of all the impassioned
speeches he had given. Here was a man fully conscious of
the burden he had assumed, yet not bowed under it. Here
was a man of courage, a man other men could trust to do his
best, with, as he had said, God's help.

The speech Lincoln gave that evening was in reality an
appeal. He beseeched the people not to look to government
for the answer to the momentous problem of the times.
"Constantly bear in mind that with you, and not with politicians, not with Presidents . . . but with you is the question:
Shall the Union and shall the Liberties of this country be
preserved." It was apparently a sobering thought, for the
crowd departed in a far less joyous mood than it had
arrived.

In his first inaugural address, delivered March 4, 1861,
Lincoln did more than hint about what his policy toward
the South was to be. He assured the South that sectional
rights would be protected: "I have no purpose directly or
indirectly to interfere with the institution of slavery in the
States where it exists." He went on to declare that secession
could not be allowed.

"Physically speaking, we cannot separate. . . . No state,
upon its own action, can lawfully get out of the Union."
But he insisted there would be no violence "unless it be
forced upon the national authority."

Benjamin Harrison considered the address "sensible and
conciliatory," one that should "spread oil upon the troubled
waters." He felt soothed enough himself to really buckle
down to work again. He was especially eager to organize
his reports of Supreme Court decisions, because their publication could mean extra money for him. He still was woe-
fully short of the funds needed to pay off debts on his house
and lot.

Wanting to be free from interruption, Ben took himself off to a basement room at the Presbyterian Church. He spent almost all his waking hours there from early March to early April, with only his reports for company.

During that same time, of course, the nation was *not* calm at all. It was seething and bubbling under that oil Ben thought Lincoln had spread.

Prior to Lincoln's inauguration, all forts and navy yards in the seceded states except Fort Pickens at Pensacola and Fort Sumter at Charleston had been occupied without incident by the newly formed Confederation. According to the Confederates, the forts became theirs the moment the states withdrew from the Union. Of course, they wanted Sumter and Pickens too, and a few days after the inauguration Confederate President Jefferson Davis sent a group of staff officers to Washington to ask for the forts' surrender. William H. Seward, Lincoln's Secretary of State, would not receive the delegates, but through a messenger he led them to believe that both forts would be soon evacuated and that until then no more supplies would be sent to the garrisons at either one.

Lincoln did not like being committed without being consulted. More important, he did not approve of evacuating such strategic strongholds. And he certainly was not going to let the garrisons go hungry. Therefore, against the advice of General of the Army Winfield Scott, against the advice too of five out of seven men of his Cabinet, Lincoln ordered relief supplies sent to the forts.

He did take the precaution of informing South Carolina on April 6 that only food was being sent to Sumter, but South Carolina feared a trick. On Friday, April 12, at 4:30 in the morning, the shore batteries at Charleston under the command of Confederate General Pierre G. T. Beauregard opened fire on Fort Sumter.

The news of what surely meant the start of a civil war

was brought to Ben in his basement retreat. Instantly he dropped his pen and rushed outside to join the milling mass that was headed for the State House. Over and over again people asked the same question of each other: "Could the small garrison at Fort Sumter hold out until help came?"

It could for only thirty-four hours. At 2:30 P.M. the next day, Major Anderson, commander of the fort, was forced to surrender. Sumter had fallen.

The thought of seventy loyal men being bombarded by thousands of rebels aroused a whirlwind of patriotism in the northern states. The eloquent Ralph Waldo Emerson expressed the northerners' sentiments:

"Now we have a country again. Sometimes gunpowder smells good."

On April 15, President Lincoln declared that "insurrection" existed and called for 75,000 three-month volunteers. This move was interpreted by the state of Virginia as the "coercion" it and other upper South states had said they would not countenance. On April 17, Virginia's convention voted 103–46 for secession. The 46 represented the mountainous western section of the state. The counties there refused to recognize secession. They were later (in June, 1863) to be admitted into the Union as a separate state, West Virginia, but for the time being they just affirmed their loyalty to the Union.

In Indianapolis during this time, Benjamin Harrison had done a lot of soul-searching, a lot of praying for guidance. The moment he heard about the firing on Fort Sumter he had, he said, "felt the fighting blood of his forefathers rush through his veins." He had wanted to start off at once to avenge those "guns of treason" that had attacked without real provocation.

He was not one to act on impulse, however. In the two days before Lincoln issued his call to arms, Ben tried to look soberly at both sides of the situation: duty to country on the one hand, civil and domestic obligations on the other.

Ben had hoped the Sunday worship service would help calm his spirit so he could think more clearly, but it did not. Prayers, hymns, the sermon—all were designed to rally Christians to the support of the "glorious cause."

Actually, it was the wording of the call to arms that made up Ben's mind for him. The President asked for three-month volunteers. Apparently he expected the rebellion would be ended by that time. In that case, Ben felt he could with a clear conscience allow others—bachelors or career soldiers—to fill the Indiana quota of six thousand men.

In spite of his decision, Ben waited anxiously to see if Indiana would indeed fill her quota. To his intense relief, the state was one of the first to do so, not with six thousand men but with double that number. Ben no longer had to feel any guilt.

Perhaps in order to make himself too tired to regret not being in the thick of things, Ben plunged intensely into work. The duties of his Supreme Court task were demanding, involving keeping and editing the detailed records of court trials and judicial decisions. In addition, Ben had obligations to his law firm, Wallace and Harrison. However, he now spent much more time at both pursuits than he needed to, and as a result his home life suffered. It was a wonder his health wasn't undermined as well, but fortunately he was blessed with an extremely rugged constitution.

The war was, of course, not over in three months, and Lincoln had to keep calling for more and more men. Each time he did, Benjamin Harrison watched Indiana's response. There seemed to be no end of men ready to answer.

In the summer of 1861, Ben's partner, Will Wallace,

decided to be a candidate again for the office of clerk of
Marion County, and he spent a great deal of time campaigning. Ben had achieved his partnership with Wallace
out of Will's first campaign, and he had been ready and
eager then to take on the extra work while Will was away.
Now circumstances were different. Ben had not the time or
the energy to satisfy both his and Will's clients for long.

The partners therefore came to an agreement. If Will
was elected in November, the partnership of Wallace and
Harrison would terminate. Ben would then seek another
partner, one who could equalize the load.

Will did win, and his partnership with Ben was dissolved.
Two weeks later, on December 11, 1861, Ben took a new
partner, a friend since Miami University days, William P.
Fishback. The new combination was excellent. "Pink"
Fishback—his middle name was Pinckney—was every bit as
hard a worker as Ben, also able to carry more than his share
of legal work if it was ever necessary.

Together the two young men quickly raised their firm
to the front rank among Indiana law offices. The ingredients
of their success were simple: conservative advice and un-
tiring devotion to each case and client they accepted.

The Union was not faring as well as the firm of Harrison
and Fishback. People had grown used to the beating of
drums and the march of soldiers' feet now. They did not
respond so quickly to appeals for volunteers. This was not
immediately apparent in Indiana, where, according to the
Secretary of War, volunteering outstripped Massachusetts
two to one. But by the summer of 1862, apathy had reached
even there. When, on the second of July, President Lincoln
called for 300,000 more volunteers, Indiana men barely
stirred.

On July 9, Ben and his former law partner, Will Wallace,
went to see Governor Morton on some state business. He

seemed to listen to what they had to say, but it was obvious that his mind was not on the matter under discussion. As soon as they could, Ben and Will concluded their comments and rose to leave.

Governor Morton detained them, asking them to step into his inner office. There he gestured toward a window, from which workmen could be seen putting up a new building, and he growled about the waste of using able-bodied men in such a pursuit, when the country was in danger of destruction. Then he explained: "Gentlemen, there is absolutely no response to Mr. Lincoln's last call for troops. The people do not appear to realize the necessities of the situation. Something must be done to break the spirit of apathy and indifference which now prevails."

Ben, hearing this plea, knew that his reasons for staying home were no longer heavy enough. His duty to his country now outweighed them.

"Governor," he said, "if I can be of any service, I will go."

Morton was silent for a few moments. Then he said, "You can raise a regiment in this district right away; but it is asking too much of you to go into the field with it. We will find somebody else to command it."

Ben would not hear of this compromise. He told the governor he would not make a recruiting speech and get men to enlist for a task he would not undertake himself.

"Well," said the governor, "then you can command it."

"I don't know as I want to," Ben said. "I have had no military experience."

So, for the time being, Morton commissioned Benjamin Harrison a second lieutenant in the Seventieth regiment, Indiana volunteers. He was fully empowered to "enlist volunteers for said regiment and muster them into the United States service."

As Will and Ben were walking out the door, Ben got his

first recruit: Will Wallace himself. Then the two young men walked straight to a store where they bought military caps. Next, Ben hired a drummer and a fifer to come play in front of his law office, which he intended to convert at once into a recruiting station. Returning to the office himself, he hung an American flag out the window and confidently waited for recruit number two of Company A.

He got recruit number two rapidly, and then a few more, but men didn't exactly rush up to enlist. So Ben reasoned it was time to stir up the fires of patriotism by more vigorous means. He hired Masonic Hall for a "grand and glorious rally of all friends of the Union" and announced not only Governor Morton, County Clerk Wallace, and himself as speakers but also the "Hero of Philippi," General Dumont.

Philippi, in northwest Virginia, was the scene of one of the first battles of the war, waged on June 3, 1861. There Union Colonel (he was made a general later) Dumont and Colonel Kelley routed Confederates and gained possession of the crucial Baltimore and Ohio Railroad.

Getting General Dumont was a shrewd move, for early victories such as his at Philippi had made deep impressions on loyal Unionists. Everybody in Indianapolis, it seemed, wanted to see him. The result was, on the evening of July 12, Masonic Hall could not hold the crowd, so a second meeting was set up in the State House grove. The speakers agreed to address both groups in turn, two starting at one place, two at the other.

The speakers did not mince words. They all hammered home the same point. *Indiana must do her duty or the country was lost.*

Faced with the example not only of the hero of Philippi but also of new volunteers Benjamin Harrison and William Wallace, who could easily have paid someone to fight in their stead, a good number of men agreed to enlist on the spot.

So the rally had helped to fill the ranks of the Seventieth Indiana regiment, but it hadn't persuaded enough men. During the week following, Ben spent every evening speech-making, managing to pick up a few recruits each night.

Then suddenly the need for speech-making was over. Indiana itself was in danger of being invaded. Already rebels were in possession of Henderson, Kentucky. Evans-ville, Indiana, was feared to be next!

The war coming that close to home was all Indianans needed to rally around the flag. On July 22, Ben was ready to file the muster roll of Company A with the adjutant general. As a reward, Governor Morton raised Ben's rank to captain.

That same evening Ben's company, along with four other newly recruited Indiana companies, reported at their camp at the old state fairgrounds.

As Ben had told Governor Morton, he knew nothing about military drill. To assure his men the best possible training, he had hired a drillmaster from Chicago, arrang-ing to pay for the service from his own pocket.

Ben himself stayed in town to tie up the few loose ends that must be secured before he could take up his new challenge.

CHAPTER 7

Harrison of the
Seventieth Indiana

BEN'S PRIMARY CONCERN was to provide for his family while
he was gone. Since his reporter's job at the Supreme Court
was an important source of extra income, he had to find a
deputy who would handle the position successfully for him.
Also, he had to know what was to become of his legal
practice.

Reluctantly, for he was tempted to enlist himself, "Pink"
Fishback agreed to stay and handle affairs at the office for
both of them. That was one loose end tied up and a major
load off Ben's mind.

In the matter of finding a deputy for himself as reporter,
Ben was blessed too. John Caven, an admirer of Ben, accepted the trust "for such proceeds from the work as would
fairly remunerate him." The pact between them was just a
gentlemen's agreement. Ben, usually such a stickler for
legality, unwisely neglected to put it in writing, leaving it
on trust. He felt sure that the last remaining loose end was
now secured, and he could get on with the business of
Company A.

When Ben joined his men in camp, he was gratified to
learn two things. First, the Seventieth Indiana regiment
was not only full but had a surplus of more than two hundred men. Second, he himself had been recommissioned as

a result, so that now he held the rank of full colonel of volunteers.

No one knew better than the young commander himself how lacking he was in military knowledge, so with his usual dedication to the job at hand, he set himself to acquiring it. He learned from the drillmaster by day. He burned candles late every night, studying theoretical tactics and the art of war.

Four days after he had assumed command, Colonel Harrison and his regiment were ordered to join the concentration of Union troops at Louisville, Kentucky. At seven in the morning of August 13, 1862, they broke camp and proceeded to the train station on foot. No doubt Ben was pleased to hear favorable comments about the soldierly bearing of his men, but he was well aware that in actuality they scarcely knew how to load their Springfield and Enfield rifles.

Ben expected that his regiment would be kept at Louisville long enough to learn such routine matters, yet twenty-four hours after their arrival they were hurried on to Bowling Green, a fortified Union center about thirty miles north of the Tennessee border. Confederate General Braxton Bragg was rumored to be north of Nashville, Tennessee. The only way to keep him from proceeding to Louisville itself was to stop him at Bowling Green.

At Bowling Green, Harrison learned that the imminent danger was not so much from General Bragg as from the guerilla fighter, John Morgan, and his band of marauding cavalry. Morgan had already destroyed railroad bridges and several sections of track at Gallatin, Tennessee, and was headed north.

The momentary possibility of actual combat made the men of the Seventieth Indiana realize that their very lives would soon depend on knowing what to do and how to do it. They concentrated on the exercises set them, and within a week a visiting general complimented Ben.

"In the promptness of movement and in soldierly appearance, the Seventieth Indiana would rival many older regiments, Colonel," he said.

Discipline was given as much attention as drill, because Ben knew character training was as important as military training. Reveille sounded at five, and each company had an hour's drill before breakfast at six. Next, two hours' more drill followed mounting guard, officers' drill, and police duty. Dinner was at twelve noon, noncommissioned officers' drill from one to two, battalion drill from two to four; after five o'clock supper, dress parade from six to seven; roll call at eight; taps at nine.

Ben was no less severe with himself than with his men; he was determined that they should not suffer because their commanding officer did not know what to command when.

His diligent study paid off the first time he was ordered on an independent expedition. A body of rebels was lodged in the vicinity of Russellville, Kentucky. On September 30, Harrison received orders to surprise and rout them.

He and his men, aboard a train of the Louisville-Nashville Railroad, progressed without incident until they were ten miles from Russellville. There, apparently thinking they would effectively prevent pursuit, the enemy had partially destroyed a bridge any train coming from the north must cross. But Harrison was stopped only temporarily. He had some railroad men in his regiment, and with them directing the others, a makeshift bridge was constructed from old railroad ties, a couple of large trees, and some track from a siding. Within three hours, the train was able to proceed slowly again. Once across, they pushed to within two miles of target. Then Colonel Harrison elected to use divide and conquer tactics. He sent four companies to come in on the other side of the town and so block any possible retreat of the rebels. He gave them time to take up their position. Then he ordered the rest of his men to attack.

The surprise was complete; the rebels had no time to prepare for action. Most of them were killed. Those who were not were taken prisoner. All their horses and arms were captured as well, and Harrison and his regiment returned to Bowling Green justifiably pleased with their success.

In the next few weeks, the Seventieth Indiana was sent off on what proved fruitless attempts to capture Morgan and his raiders. This chafed Ben Harrison in particular, because he was at the same time powerless to do anything about a political dispute developing back in Indianapolis.

Back home, Indiana Democrats were maintaining that Harrison had no right to the office of Supreme Court reporter while he was also in the pay of the U.S. Army. They claimed that, according to the state constitution, no person was permitted to hold two "lucrative" government positions. They were instituting court action to have his elective post declared vacant.

In reality, of course, Harrison's army commission was *not* lucrative. He relied upon the Supreme Court job for the partial support of his family. His only hope of keeping it, however, lay in the willingness of Indiana Republicans to fight the home-front battle for him. From where he was, he was unable to do more than hope.

If the Republicans tried, they did not try hard enough. The court declared the reportership vacant, to be filled in the coming October, 1862, election.

Hearing that, Ben wrote to the Central Committee of the Republican Party and asked that John Caven, as his deputy, be nominated to run against whomever the Democrats should select. The committee, however, replied that there was "no proof" that Caven was in truth a deputy, and they preferred to choose another candidate.

Now, when it was too late, Ben realized how negligent he

had been in making only a gentleman's agreement with Caven. He had done a disservice not only to himself but to Caven. Now Caven was without a job, no matter which party won the coveted post.

It may have been weakness on Ben's part, but perhaps he could not be too harshly blamed for a comment he was heard to make: "All traitors are not found in the military."

Letters telling of unrest at home upset Harrison's troops as well as Ben himself. When they read about Indiana's hostile reaction to Lincoln's preliminary proclamation of emancipation, some of them began to wonder why they should be risking their necks while "soreheads" sniped with words. When the October elections ousted the majority of Republicans and men who were on record as being opposed to the war took office instead, the troops became even more disturbed.

A Democrat was elected to fill Ben's job as reporter of the Supreme Court, but Ben had no time to brood about that now. He knew he had to boost his men's morale, or they would be worthless as a fighting unit. Remembering how successful a rally had been when he needed recruits, he now organized another one to include the entire regiment and asked all the leaders to speak.

It was a shrewd plan, for the speakers tried to outdo each other in proclaiming loyalty to the Union cause. They told the troops that the Union victory in the bloody battle of Antietam, which had given Lincoln the courage to issue his preliminary emancipation proclamation, had also had "immeasurably important repercussions" abroad. The British and French governments, which had been on the verge of recognizing the Confederacy, had instead held back.

"Isn't that proof enough, lads, that right's on our side?" asked Ben.

He was greeted by enthusiastic applause and even the affectionate rejoinder: "You tell 'em, Little Ben!"

The mass meeting was the success Ben had hoped it would be, but now he wished they could get into some exciting action that would make use of the men's reawakened loyalty.

Toward the end of the month, he had reason to hope the chance would come very soon. General William S. Rosecrans was placed in command of an enlarged area known as the Department of the Cumberland. This could only mean that a big push into the Deep South was contemplated, and if so, Harrison and his Hoosiers would be expected to participate.

On October 30, General Rosecrans established headquarters at Louisville and on November 2 came to the encampment at Bowling Green. There he announced a tripartite division of his army. Three divisions were assigned to each wing, five to the center. The Seventieth Indiana was brigaded with an Ohio and three Illinois regiments at the center, with Brigadier General W. T. Ward of Kentucky in command.

A week later the Seventieth Indiana was ordered to Scottsville, Kentucky, a three-day march. The officers had horses to ride, but the soldiers had to walk, and many of them were not up to the effort. An epidemic of dysentery had recently raged through the camp, leaving those who had suffered from it very weak. Ben kept a watchful eye on his men, and a number of times he dismounted in order to let a weary soldier ride. This kindness was noted by the regiment and greatly increased Ben's popularity with the men.

The vicinity of Scottsville proved a poor place for a camp. There was no stretch of level ground big enough to allow drilling exercise, and the men grew restless with nothing active to do. All were glad when the brigade was ordered on to Gallatin, Tennessee. Perhaps *now* they'd see action, for Confederate General Bragg's forces were near Murfreesboro, not too far away.

Some of the brigade was soon to get this wish, but not

Harrison and his men. In mid-December General Rosecrans assigned them to guard the twenty-six miles of railroad from Gallatin to Nashville. Rosecrans considered the duty extremely important, because the railroad was the lifeline to the base of supplies, but Ben and his men were very disappointed.

The Battle of Murfreesboro began three days later. The Seventieth Indiana, from their relatively safe post, could hear the heavy bombing of artillery in the distance, and all the men on routine picket and guard duty felt anguish at not being able to participate.

The engagement ended in a Union triumph. Bragg and his forces were so completely crushed that rebellion in the West (as this area was thought of) almost ceased for six months. Consequently, the military operations of the entire Army of the Cumberland were as routine as those of the Seventieth Indiana.

In February, 1863, while yet on guard over the railroad, Ben heard of the death of his grandmother, Mrs. William Henry Harrison, and he was saddened. He had been a favorite of hers, he knew. She had time and again charged him to be sure to "live up to the grand name of Benjamin."

Ben was the sixth of that name in America. The first Benjamin Harrison had emigrated from England in 1635 and settled in Surry County, Virginia, just across the James River from Jamestown. The fifth, also of Virginia, had been the Ben of the American Revolution, Benjamin the signer of the Declaration of Independence.

Perhaps the sixth Benjamin wondered ruefully if he'd ever do anything militarily important enough so that later generations would call *him* the Ben of the Civil War. Certainly, he hadn't so far in the six months he'd been in the army!

He was frustrated by not being able to accomplish something for the cause he came to fight for, Ben was heard to mutter. Of course, he was forgetting the old adage about "they also serve who only stand and wait." He did what he was asked to do, and did it well. He also kept drilling his men with regularity and studying military books himself. W. J. Hardee's *Rifle and Light Infantry Tactics* became his second Bible. Ben also read all accounts he could find of celebrated campaigns and battles of history, including all of Napoleon's campaigns, and studied treatises on field fortifications. He drew diagrams of methods of laying out, constructing, defending and attacking different kinds of entrenchments. He also insisted that the other officers study. He made a habit of questioning them on what they had read and requiring them to illustrate maneuvers on a blackboard.

The prowess of Ben and the men under his command did not go unnoticed by his superior officers. One of them, Major General Brigney, said, "Your unit takes the shine of all the brigade in mounting, in dress parade, and in battalion drill."

Ben's theory was that every day in camp should be used as preparation for that other day—the day of battle.

At last, on January 2, 1864, after a year and a half of minor assignments, Harrison and his men were called to the front. There they became part of the First Brigade of the Twentieth Army Corps. This was the outfit in which the Seventieth Indiana was to serve until the end of the war. At the time, General William T. Ward was the brigade commander.

Important changes in military position were being made in Washington, too. On March 9, 1864, General Ulysses S. Grant became Supreme Commander of the Union Forces, General William Tecumseh Sherman second in command. Grant would be directing the main armies in the east, Sherman in the west.

With them in charge, the strategy of the North was no longer to be "hit or miss." Both Grant and Sherman were trained professional soldiers, and they could be expected not to make a move that hadn't been thoroughly plotted in advance.

Grant's plan was to use battering-ram tactics on southern troops in Virginia and so place the Chief Commander of the Confederate Army, Robert E. Lee, on the defensive in Richmond. Sherman's task was to go after the army of Confederate General Joseph E. Johnston, and above all to keep Johnston so busy he could not spare any of his men to go to the aid of Lee.

Sherman spent two months rearranging the 100,000 men under his command into three strong but varisized armies: the Army of the Ohio, the Army of the Tennessee, and the Army of the Cumberland. The last, led by Major General George H. Thomas, was the largest, with 61,000 men. The Twentieth Army Corps, including Harrison's regiment, was part of it.

General Grant had finally set May 5, 1864, as the day for him and Sherman to start their simultaneous maneuvers against Lee and Johnston. On that day Sherman's three armies moved out from their headquarters at Chattanooga, Tennessee, and started the now memorable march through Georgia.

Johnston was entrenched in Resaca, a town in northwest Georgia, and around it he had formed a horseshoe-shaped defense line. Natural defenses about the town were also formidable—hills, swamps, ravines, and the densest of thickets. Undoubtedly, Johnston felt any attack on this stronghold by Union forces would be, if not impossible, at least suicidal.

On May 15, the attack began. At once rebel batteries, perched on the crest of a hill commanding the approach to the town, poured incessant fire into the Union ranks. Ob-

President-elect Harrison in his Indianapolis library with Vice-President-elect Levi P. Morton

President Harrison reviewing his Inaugural Day Parade

A cartoon of Harrison and the many applications for Cabinet positions

JEREMIAH McLAIN RUSK.

WILLIAM WINDOM.

JAMES G. BLAINE.

WILLIAM HENRY HARRISON MILLER.

JOHN WILLOCK NOBLE.

BENJAMIN FRANKLIN TRACY.

JOHN WANAMAKER.

REDFIELD PROCTOR.

President Harrison and his Cabinet

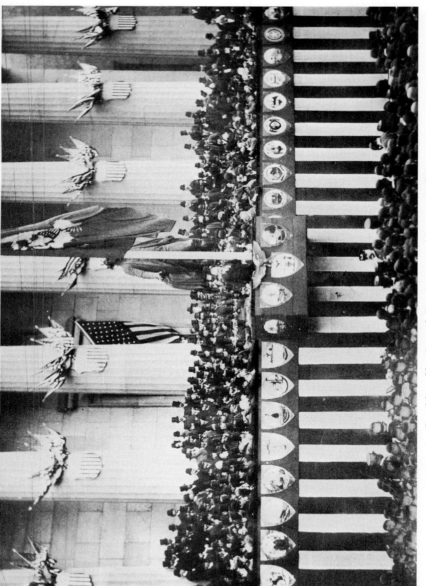

President Harrison delivering an address in 1889

President Harrison salutes the Centennial procession from the reviewing stand on Madison Square

President and Mrs. Harrison

President Harrison's official photograph

viously, for the Union troops it was necessary to silence those guns, no matter what the cost.

The order to do so came filtering through the various levels of command to General William Ward's brigade. Ward, in turn, issued orders to Harrison. At a signal, the Seventieth Indiana was to storm the hill and knock out the rebel guns.

Ben now faced his first important assignment under fire. He saw at once that the pine woods were impenetrable by horseback, so he ordered all officers to dismount. Then, himself in the lead, he shouted, "Come on, boys!" and charged.

The men crashed into the forest after him, shouting "Forward!" to each other. They soon emerged from the shelter of the trees, to be met by murderous fire. An account of the times says: "Shot and shell flew thick about the brave leader. Still he went on—on through the smoke and terrible din. Men fell fast, and there was no time to carry them to the rear; scarcely time to avoid trampling the wounded to death."

At last they reached the outer Confederate redoubt, and Harrison was the first to leap over the parapet. Hand-to-hand combat ensued, Ben's men using their muskets like clubs, until all the rebels who were not killed were taken prisoner.

Possibly it was this successful action that made General Johnston realize that his position in Resaca was not impregnable. Anyway, that same night under cover of darkness, he and his command retreated across the Oostenaula River. Resaca was left free for occupation by Union troops.

Since securing Resaca was the first step in the campaign toward the capture of Atlanta, Sherman might have been happy. But he was not. He was bitterly disappointed that Johnston and the main body of his Confederate troops had escaped. Grimly, he declared, "We will hound Johnston until he is trapped."

In consequence, after Resaca, Ben quickly took part in a

series of other battles. In one month he was engaged in more battles than William Henry Harrison or Andrew Jackson fought in their entire lives.

It was Harrison's actions in the Battle of Peach Tree Creek on July 20, 1864, that won him eventual promotion to the rank of Brigadier General of Volunteers. Ward's division was not expected to get into active fighting there; in fact, the regiments comprising that division had been ordered to stay some distance to the rear of the rest of the army. However, Confederate General Hood apparently thought he would use that quarter mile between as a wedge to cut Sherman's lines in two.

Astonishingly, even after firing started, General Ward could not believe the Confederate Army was really taking the initiative. He would not give the order to close the gap. So Harrison decided he would have to take the initiative himself.

An eyewitness account in the Indianapolis *Daily Journal* reported Harrison as saying: "Come on, boys, we're not licked yet. . . . We haven't much ammunition, but if necessary we can give them the cold steel. . . . Come on!" Then, leading the men on the double-quick, he dashed up the slope.

The same *Journal* account quotes one of Ben's men as saying, "But for Harrison, I think our army would have been cut in two, and at least one wing of it badly shattered."

On August 20, 1864, Ben became thirty-one years old, and he found himself fervently hoping he'd be a private citizen again before another birthday rolled around. He knew there was no question of even a furlough until Atlanta fell into Union hands, and at the moment the possibility of that event seemed remote. As soon as the Union troops gained one position, the enemy had another all ready.

Then, suddenly, Sherman instituted a series of brilliant

maneuvers which took the Union Army close to Atlanta. On September 1, the Confederates were forced to evacuate it.

Shortly afterwards General Sherman decreed that his troops had earned a rest. Colonel Harrison received an order to "report in person to the Honorable O. P. Morton, Governor of Indiana, at Indianapolis, Indiana, for special duty."

Ben had no inkling of what that special duty would be, but it really didn't matter. He was going to Indianapolis; he was going home!

CHAPTER 8

The First
Post-War Years

NEWS NOT ONLY of General William Tecumseh Sherman's capture of Atlanta but also of General Phil Sheridan's victory in the Valley of the Shenandoah had reached Indianapolis before Ben returned there. In consequence, talk about an "unnecessary war" and "ousting Lincoln" had ceased. Instead, the citizens had nothing but praise for the Union cause.

This attitude augured well for Lincoln's chances of re-election. It also encouraged local Republicans to believe they could dump the Democrats out of the state offices they had won two years before.

Ben was aware that he had been renominated by the state convention for the office of reporter of the Supreme Court. The information had reached him while he was stationed in Tennessee. He had replied that he would be "gratified to resume the duties of reporter if the war was over or virtually so," but that he would not quit the army for any civil office or pursuit, unless incapacitated for service.

In line with his devotion to his army service, Ben was quick to carry out Sherman's most recent orders to him. He reported to Governor Morton to learn what special duty was to be his.

The duty was very much to his taste. After enjoying a

short period of rest and relaxation with his family, he was to do two things: first, he was to support his own candidacy and his party by electioneering; second, he was to canvass the state for army recruits.

Actually, he was able to kill two birds with one stone. As the hero of Resaca and Peach Tree Creek, he was able just by appearing in person to accomplish a great deal before he opened his mouth.

When the state election was held on October 11, 1864, both Morton and Harrison won by 20,000 votes. In fact, the Republicans rewon control of the General Assembly and elected eight of the eleven contested congressional seats as well.

Ben's electioneering in the interests of Lincoln was even more intense than it had been for himself and Morton. He defended the President's Emancipation Proclamation, made January 1, 1863, saying that it "did but reflect the will of the people." To back up this statement, he gave personal testimony to the wisdom of it. He declared that "not a Negro escaped and made his way into our camps but has brought more aid to our cause than the entire brood of whining, carping Copperheads who object to the employment of black men."

"Copperheads" were northerners who sympathized with the South during the Civil War. Harrison was well aware that it had been such "treasonable men" who were responsible for stirring up trouble for the Union cause in Indiana —who had been the reason for the letters from home that had upset his men when in camp in Kentucky.

Now, with the Union armies so recently victorious, Ben's words were received with wild enthusiasm. And on November 7, Indiana went as wildly to vote for Lincoln at the polls, greatly contributing to his landslide victory.

Governor Morton was loud in his praise of Ben's elo-

quence, commending him for the way he had acted in and
beyond the call of duty. Now that the particular job he'd
been assigned was over, though, Morton didn't know what
to order Ben to do next: stay and carry out his reporter
duties or return to the front.

Ben solved the dilemma by requesting permission to
return, so Morton wrote up the order, to take effect at once.

"At once" was the day after the presidential election, and
on that day Ben started off by train to rejoin his regiment at
Atlanta. He got as far as Dalton, Georgia, only to find the
railroad torn up and further progress by road impossible.
But for this turn of fortune, Benjamin Harrison would have
participated in Sherman's celebrated March to the Sea. As
it was, he was ordered instead to report to General Charles
Cruft at Chattanooga and take command of a brigade.

Harrison had barely reached Chattanooga before General Thomas called for help in preventing the Confederates
under General Hood from taking Nashville. Hood was expected to strike at the end of the first week of December,
but the weather turned bitterly cold. The earth became a
sheet of ice, so it was virtually impossible to move artillery
and cavalry.

The suffering of the soldiers during this time was intense.
Some of them died on the picket lines, and a great many
were so frostbitten they never recovered. Harrison, as
always, felt a great responsibility for his men, and he did
what he could to alleviate their discomfort. At night he
walked the picket lines himself, serving the men hot coffee.
This special act of kindness was one reason Little Ben was
remembered with affection by veterans in the postwar
years.

The Battle of Nashville finally began at dawn on December 15, 1864, and winning it was a great feather in the cap
of the Union forces. The Confederates were not only driven
away from Nashville but out of Tennessee altogether.

This put an end to war in that state, and practically in the West. On New Year's Eve the campaign finally ended, and Harrison was ordered to report back to General Cruft in Chattanooga.

There, on January 16, 1865, Harrison finally received orders to proceed without delay to Savannah, Georgia, and rejoin his proper command. This delighted Ben, for he felt he belonged with the Seventieth Indiana as long as the regiment was in the field.

However, his reunion with his men was delayed again, this time by an attack of scarlet fever. Ben was dangerously ill for several weeks, and as he was recovering he was still too weak to appreciate the news that his promotion to brigadier general had come through. Still, there it was: signed by Abraham Lincoln and countersigned by E. W. Stanton, Secretary of War, the commission stated that it was given "for ability and manifest energy and gallantry in command of the brigade." Ben was now entitled to be called General Harrison.

When Harrison was finally well enough to resume command, he took a ship for Wilmington, North Carolina. Arriving there on April 12, he learned belatedly that General Robert E. Lee had surrendered to General Grant at Appomattox three days before.

The back of the South was bowed but not quite broken, and Ben was still eager to get back to his command, which he had left at the end of the Atlanta campaign six months before. On April 19, he finally made it.

He had been anticipating that the moment would be joyous, but when he arrived at the Raleigh encampment, scarcely anyone had spirit to do more than acknowledge his presence. General Sherman had just issued a delayed bulletin: President Lincoln had been shot on April 14 and had died of his wounds on April 15.

Why had Sherman waited to announce Lincoln's death?

Probably because he feared it would adversely affect the peace negotiations he was making with Johnston. Johnston's surrender had come about the day before, Ben learned, but the joy the troops would naturally feel was instantly overshadowed by tragedy. Many soldiers wanted to do just what Sherman had feared: hit out violently, armistice or no armistice. Of course, they were restrained by their officers from taking action.

Southern resistance didn't end completely until May 26, when Confederate General Kirby Smith capitulated to General Canby at New Orleans. Before that time, however, Sherman's army was on the march to Washington to join the grand review of Union troops.

The great military spectacle thrilled the nation's capital for two days. On Tuesday, May 23, the East had its day, as each unit of the eastern army marched by the wooden stand where President Andrew Johnson and his Cabinet stood, flanked by governors, congressmen, and celebrities from every part of the Union.

On Wednesday, Sherman's army took the limelight. To the strains of "The Star-Spangled Banner" the westerners marched in perfect time. Sherman himself later admitted he was thrilled when, stealing a glance backward at his troops, he saw "legions coming in line, every man locked in steady formation—formal for perhaps the first and last time in their lives."

Ben was proud enough of his men, he said, to burst his buttons. What an anticlimax it was to have to stay in Washington for three weeks after that glorious day, when all he wanted to do was get home! But it took that long to cut all the red tape connected with mustering-out papers. Not until June 8, 1865, did he receive the discharge document restoring him to the role of civilian.

As Ben and his regiment prepared to leave for home, they

might well have been thinking of Sherman's farewell words to his army: "As in war you have been good soldiers, so in peace you will be good citizens." Certainly, they looked forward to taking up a normal life again.

The friends and relatives of Company A, Seventieth Indiana, were not ready to let them become "just citizens" right away. They were greeted at the station as conquering heroes and for a week were honored at receptions and parties. Most of the returned soldiers were embarrassed at being so much in the limelight and honestly looked forward to being allowed to fade into the background again.

Benjamin Harrison was glad to get back to the routine of business life. In his absence, but with his consent, a third partner had been added to his law firm. Albert G. Porter was a long-time friend of Ben's, and Ben was pleased to be associated with him in this new way. Besides, with three lawyers sharing the legal load, Ben hoped he would not have to work such long hours as he had before the war. He wanted to have more leisure to be with his family, whom he had missed very much. His son and daughter had been scarcely more than babies when he entered the army. Now they were eleven and eight, and he didn't feel he knew them at all.

Ben did, of course, have to take up the duties of reporter again, too. This time the deputy he had selected to fill in for him between his election on October, 1864, and his military discharge had been allowed to function. The deputy had, in fact, done such an admirable job that he was able to hand Ben page proofs of all the Supreme Court decisions ready for publication, from which Ben derived considerable extra income. The volumes were much in demand by lawyers and state officials throughout Indiana.

Many problems confronted the Union after the war, the major one undoubtedly being the reconstruction of the South. How should the ex-Confederate states be treated?

Two constitutional issues were involved: first, were the rebellious states in the Union or not; second, was the President or the Congress responsible for direction of Reconstruction?

Lincoln had maintained that the states were in the Union, because their secession had been illegal. He had also felt that it was the right of the Executive to decide how to fit them in place again. He had recommended (1) pardons for southerners taking a prescribed loyalty oath, and (2) executive recognition of state governments when ten percent of the 1860 electorate had taken the oath and when the state agreed to emancipation.

The Republican-controlled Congress disagreed with Lincoln (and with Johnson, who favored Lincoln's plan). It held that (1) the ex-Confederate states were "conquered provinces," (2) they had no state governments, and (3) Congress alone could restore them to the Union and impose such conditions for readmission as it deemed necessary.

Benjamin Harrison was as radical in his thinking as any of the Republican congressmen, and perhaps with clearer reason. He showed no sympathy either for the defeated southerners or with southern sympathizers in the North. Indiana had sent 200,000 men to war; 25,000 had never returned. Should their sacrifice be so easily forgotten?

So that there would be no doubt how he stood on the issue, Ben made many speeches explaining his stand. He was also critical of the "hard-hearted, grasping men" who often had taken advantage of the absent soldiers, even in some cases seizing their little homesteads, removing the means of livelihood to which they had expected to return. He warned repeatedly of the dangers of "placing treacherous Democrats in political power again."

Some people openly wondered how a good Presbyterian like Ben could take such an unchristian attitude. He replied: "There should be no forgiveness without repentance, and I have seen no genuine effort at self-repentance either among northern or southern rebels."

Another important question was that of Negro suffrage. Governor Morton, Republican leader in Indiana, suggested that there ought to be a "period of probation and preparation" before the four million slaves just freed from bondage should be allowed to vote.

Benjamin Harrison took a more definite stand. He said he was not in favor of letting the Negro vote yet *if the rebels were also kept from voting*. He added, "If, in the course of two or three years we can't get a loyal white population down there, then we'll take a black one."

For two years Harrison kept on speaking, practicing law, and discharging his reportorial duties. It brought him political recognition and professional and financial triumph. But it also played havoc with his health. In April, 1867, he collapsed from overwork.

Carrie nursed him back to health and then talked him into taking his first vacation since the war. The Harrisons rented a cabin by a Minnesota lake. There Ben enjoyed hunting and fishing and just plain relaxing with his family. As he returned from the hunt with squirrels or from angling with a good catch of fish, he was reminded of his childhood days, when he'd supplied such things for Grandmother Harrison's table.

He had time too to think about how he had undermined his health and what he could do to prevent such a thing again. He decided that the trouble stemmed from trying to do everything in connection with his business himself. There was no reason in the world, now that he had the money, why he could not hire someone to do routine work for him, such work as he himself had done for Bellamy Storer during his apprentice days in Cincinnati.

When he returned to Indianapolis, he hired two clerks. The time they saved him was truly amazing, and so were the benefits to him and to his family.

In line with his determination to take things easier, Ben deliberately limited his public appearances during the next year. But that didn't mean he wasn't interested in what was going on politically. Indiana took a leading part in General Grant's first campaign for the Presidency, and both Ben's law partners were avid Republican spokesmen. Ben made only one speech, at Kent, Indiana, in mid-August. He spoke of Grant's glorious military record, contrasting it with the "treasonable activities" of the Democrats during the war. It was a prize example of the sort of speech known colloquially as "waving the bloody shirt," a tactic of recalling the recent civil conflict used with success then and for years to come.

Newspapers reporting the speech said, "General Harrison is without question one of the ablest speakers in the West," and Ben's fellow Republicans congratulated him, too. Word of it even got to General Grant, and the next President of the United States wrote to thank him wholeheartedly.

The following February, 1869, Ben won legal laurels as attorney for the prosecution in one of the century's most sensational murder trials, later written up in detail in a little book called *The Cold Springs Tragedy*.

The twin homicide of Jacob and Nancy Young had taken place in September, 1868. In October, a young woman named Nancy Clem, who witnesses said had been seen riding in a buggy with the Youngs on the afternoon of the crime, was arrested and later indicted for their murder. The firm of Porter, Harrison, and Fishback was appointed to assist the state.

The appointment came at a bad time for Ben. He had recently been asked to serve as one of a committee of five lawyers assigned to study the inadequacies of the Indianapolis court system. This meant he had to spend hours delving into the records of federal, county, and common plea courts.

Albert Porter, too, was up to his neck in the political maneuverings attending Grant's presidential campaign. Therefore, "Pink" Fishback for the time being had to carry most of the work on the Clem case. His partners would, of course, spend as many hours in court as possible during the giving of testimony. Also, they would be available for consultation.

One hundred and fifty witnesses gave contradictory testimony. When the case finally went to the jury on December 1, the members were unable to agree on a verdict. So they were dismissed and a new trial was scheduled for February.

Now Ben was at last free to really study the case. The work of the Committee of Five was done. Also, he had resigned from his reporter's office, since he was now financially secure enough not to need the money that publishing the *Reports* brought in.

During the first trial, the defense lawyers had produced two witnesses to swear that Nancy Clem was at home during the time she was alleged to be out riding with the Youngs. The state would have to prove the witnesses lied, or it had no case.

Ben set about cross-examining the defense witnesses with care that showed how meticulously he had studied every word they had said on the stand. He showed where they had made statements contradicting themselves. He probed and he dissected, and he finally got one of the two, Mrs. Clem's young niece, to confess that her aunt had forced her to lie.

At that point, Ben turned to the jury and said, "I do not know which is the worst criminal: the man who takes the life of his fellow, or he who saps the foundation of childish innocence and truth."

He did not say, but he certainly let the jury think, that

Mrs. Clem was doubly a fiend for she was guilty of both crimes.

This time when the case went to the jury, the members did agree on a verdict: guilty as charged. Mrs. Clem was sentenced to life imprisonment for committing murder in the second degree.

First degree murder would have meant hanging. Ben, who was a kindhearted man, was probably relieved that even a "doubly guilty" woman should not have to suffer that fate.

The newspapers, which had carried every detail of the long courtroom battle, now had only the highest praise for Harrison's efforts as public prosecutor. So did lawyers from all over the state, who had read about him or heard him personally. As for Ben's fellow Republicans, they took note of all the favorable credits Benjamin Harrison was storing up. *Their* verdict: Young Harrison was a man to keep a political eye on.

CHAPTER 9

Precarious Politics

THE YEARS OF 1869, 1870, and 1871 were relatively quiet and peaceful for Ben and his family. Now that he had only his law practice to occupy his energies, Ben could spend more time "just living." He grew to enjoy working with Carrie in the yard, planting fruit trees and flowering shrubs. He also had more chances to be with the veterans of the Seventieth Indiana and enjoyed swapping stories of the war with them.

In mid-June, 1870, "Pink" Fishback resigned from his partnership with Harrison and Porter to become editor of the Indianapolis *Journal.* In the fall, Cyrus C. Hines stepped down from his position as Civil Circuit Court Judge to take Fishback's place in the law firm. Ben found his new partner extremely congenial, perhaps because they had so much in common. Hines, too, had left a law practice to enter the army, had been promoted to the rank of colonel, and was as staunch a Republican as Ben himself.

Ben must have heard political whisperings to the effect that certain Republicans wanted him as the nominee for governor of Indiana in 1872, but he gave no sign of awareness throughout 1871. He did read with concern Fishback's editorials in the *Journal,* however, and worried about Fishback's charges of fraud and corruption within the Grant administration. He agreed with Fishback that it was essential for the party to put up first-class candidates who would champion reform.

In this he was, whether he knew it or not, placing himself in company with the fast-developing splinter group of Republicans, men who called themselves Liberal or Reform Republicans.

Then in early January, 1872, the idea of Harrison for governor got a push through various letters published in the *Journal*. They all stressed Ben's unquestionable integrity, his legal and his military proficiency. One said that all you had to do was ask the soldier boys about Little Ben. They'd tell you that "Little Ben has both the courage and the ability to meet and rout, and that the 'cat-skinners,' the hangers-on, and the political tricksters would find cold comfort in his presence, if elected."

Now Ben could not pretend that he didn't know about the wish of at least some people that he run for governor. Nevertheless, he did not know whether, if asked, he should do so or not. In the first place, he feared that campaign travel might make him overly tired again and thus ruin the health he had just managed to rebuild. In the second place, he knew that the salary of the governor of Indiana did not compare well with what he could make in private practice. Since he was the main financial support not only of his immediate family but also of his brother Irwin, who was ill with tuberculosis, and in addition he was paying tuition and buying clothes for younger brothers, this was an important consideration.

For help in his dilemma, Ben turned to his father. John Harrison introduced still another factor for him to consider. "In making up your mind as to the candidacy, I would make the chance of success a very present matter for consideration." Obviously, John Harrison had ambitious political dreams for his son, and he did not want him to make a false step if that step could be avoided.

Ben decided that he would make no public statement to the effect that he was seeking the nomination, but he told his friends privately that he would accept it if it were offered to him. This was enough of a go-ahead for William Fishback, who day after day endorsed his former law partner in the pages of the Indianapolis *Journal*. Other newspapers, knowing the intimacy between Fishback and Harrison, took this as evidence that Ben was "available" and treated him as a candidate. But there were fully declared candidates, too. Prominent among them were General Thomas McLelland Browne, now United States attorney for the district of Indiana, and Congressman Godlove Orth.

Both Browne and Orth campaigned briskly for themselves up to the February day when the nominating convention assembled in Indianapolis. Then they set up headquarters in the Bates House Hotel and continued to "blow their own horns."

When Ben made no move even so close to the wire, his friends were upset. Some were even downright angry. Didn't Harrison realize how important it was to meet the delegates, to let them see what sort of man he was? Why, some of them had the idea that he was too high-hat to be willing to come down and shake hands with them!

There seems to be no doubt that Ben's aloofness did indeed cost him the nomination. The night before the election, all sorts of detrimental comments were made about him and, Harrison not being there to answer them, were believed by the delegates who did not know him. He was termed "cold-blooded as a fish," "a stuffy aristocrat who never recognized men on the street." The consensus was men would be afraid to visit the State House with their hats on, with such a man for governor. The people wanted a man like themselves.

The poor showing he made at the state convention must have hurt Ben's self-esteem, but he was careful not to let the fact be obvious. He promised to help campaign for the successful nominee, General Browne, "as time allows."

Time didn't allow much, but Ben did make the opening speech of the Republican state campaign on July 19, 1872, and another one, even better received, five days later. His able and efficient manner of speaking was in sharp contrast to the bumbling, rambling comments of Thomas Browne. Sometimes, too, General Browne "over-indulged in the cup that cheers," so that he had to be helped up and down from the platform.

Early in August, Ben took his family away on vacation, and when he returned he found that his political fortunes had been boosted. People were disgusted with Thomas Browne. They were asking why he'd gotten the nod instead of a sober, high-minded man like Harrison.

Such talk was salve for Ben's still-wounded ego, but it was harmful to the Republican Party's hopes of winning the governorship in October, 1872. Browne did indeed lose to his Democratic opponent, Thomas Hendricks, although otherwise Republicans swept easily into the state posts. In the November election, the national Republican ticket of Grant and Wilson carried Indiana handily and also put Oliver P. Morton into the United States Senate.

In the spring of 1873, Albert Porter resigned from the law firm, so now it was Harrison and Hines. For a time they carried on alone, but there was too much business for two men to handle. They started looking around for a new third partner and finally found a suitable one in April, 1874. He was William Henry Harrison Miller, formerly of Fort Wayne, whom Ben had observed practicing in the federal court at Indianapolis. Miller quickly became a friend of Ben's and later was to serve President Harrison as his Attorney General.

For Harrison, Hines, and Miller, 1874 was a good year,

precisely because it was a bad year for a lot of other people. Back in September, 1873, the United States had fallen into a deep depression, caused by unbridled railroad speculation and overexpansion in industry, agriculture, and commerce. Financial panic followed when the powerful banking firm of Jay Cooke and Company failed. Security prices fell, and so did national income. There was widespread unemployment.

Indiana was badly hit by the national panic. Men defaulted on payments, businesses went bankrupt. And it was for these reasons that Harrison and his partners were so busy. They handled hundreds of mortgage foreclosures and bankruptcy cases.

Ben, in fact, realized an unusually good income in 1874, so that he and Carrie could at last think of building their own house. It was to be a commodious two-story red brick house, standing back in a 200-foot yard. It still stands today and is preserved as the President Benjamin Harrison Memorial Home, on North Delaware Street, Indianapolis.

Ben and Carrie took great delight in supervising the erection of their home, and with that and his exceedingly busy law practice, Ben didn't have much time to spare for politics. He could not ignore the talk of "Morton for President in '76" that was becoming louder and louder, however.

Ben had known Oliver P. Morton for a long time, and in recent years he had realized that Morton wasn't above wheeling and dealing to get what he wanted. Ben did not have evidence that Morton was *dis*honest, but there was an odor about him that Ben did not like. Therefore, Ben could not feel that Morton was the "man whose honesty was above reproach" whom the Republicans needed as their presidential candidate.

If the Republicans did not come up with such a candidate,

their chances of winning the White House again in 1876 were slim indeed. The cry against corruption in President Grant's regime was widespread.

Indiana politicians were aware that Ben did not favor Morton, but they argued that the Republican Party's needs and desires should outweigh "personal pique," which is what they thought Ben's motivation was. Indeed, they thought it would be good for everybody concerned if Harrison would run for governor. With him and Morton at the top of the slate, talk of their estrangement would have to stop.

But Ben would not consider such an arrangement, and Morton seemed pleased. This gave him a chance to back a man he knew was on his side: Godlove Orth.

The state convention of February, 1876, was thus cut and dried. The delegates endorsed Morton for the Presidency, promising to present his name to the National Convention the following June. They also unanimously nominated Orth for governor, even though he was presently Grant's minister to Austria and had not even been consulted.

The Democrats gathered in state convention in April and picked a political unknown as their gubernatorial candidate: James D. Williams. He was a Lincolnesque kind of man, tall, ugly, and extremely humble. Though really financially well-to-do, Williams usually wore denim overalls, thus earning the folksy nickname "Blue Jeans."

After the local slates had been chosen, Indianans followed the national picture with intense interest. Republicans had four avowed presidential aspirants: Morton of Indiana, James G. Blaine of Maine, Benjamin Bristow of Kentucky, and Roscoe Conkling of New York. Of them all, Bristow was the only one who was not tarred with some of the same taint of corruption as Grant. But none of them was to get the nod for the Presidency. Instead, it went to a dark horse candidate, Rutherford B. Hayes, three times governor of Ohio and an indisputably honest man.

Democrats picked Samuel J. Tilden, a reform champion, for their presidential candidate, and Indiana's present governor, Thomas A. Hendricks, for Vice-president.

Ben was pleased with the choice of Hayes, and yet he could find no objection to Tilden. It did seem that, no matter who was elected, the federal government would again be in honest hands.

Early in July, Ben left town in company with some good friends to spend a few weeks at a fishing camp. In August, Carrie and the children would join him for a relaxing family vacation, so all in all Ben planned to be away from Indianapolis most of the summer.

He had scarcely departed before the political situation in Indiana began to get as hot as the July weather. Reform-minded Republicans demanded that Godlove Orth explain his rumored connection with a group of swindlers known as the "Venezuela Ring."

The "Ring" referred to the United States representatives who in 1866 had signed a treaty with Venezuela for the settlement of unspecified claims. The Venezuelans had acted in good faith, but apparently the American representatives intended to take a percentage of all claims paid for themselves. Orth—then a congressman—was suspected of assisting the graft-minded Americans in collecting their percentages. If he had in fact done so, he was as much of a swindler as the others.

Democrats as well as Reform Republicans wanted to hear Orth's reply. When he didn't make one, his political opponents quickly labeled him unworthy of public office. Before long, even Morton came to believe that Orth was a liability to the party. Not too gently, Orth was asked to withdraw from the gubernatorial race.

On August 2, 1876, Orth finally announced his withdrawal. On August 4, the Republican Central Committee voted unanimously to replace him with Benjamin Harrison, even though Ben was not available for consultation.

When the news caught up with Ben, he refused to commit himself immediately. In a wire to the committee, he said he would seriously consider the matter and would reply at an early day.

On the day that he returned to Indianapolis, he was greeted as he had been when he returned victorious from war. He was obviously moved by the demonstration, but he in essence repeated what he had said in his wire.

"I am not ready to say to you tonight what my answer will be . . . there are some matters in connection with this that will require time for thought and consultation with my friends. But let me thank you for the expression of your good will toward me; words are inadequate to express my feelings."

The matters he had to think about included the fact that, if elected, he would have to give up his pleasant, lucrative law practice; the uncertainty as to how Morton felt about Orth's withdrawal; and how good his chances of winning were. He had clearly not forgotten his rejection in 1872 and was not to be pushed into anything.

The next day was Sunday, so Ben took his dilemma to church and there prayed for guidance. Later that day, many telegrams were delivered to him. Among them was one from Senator Morton. It said: "I congratulate you upon your nomination for governor and hope you will accept. I have no doubt of your election." So that, presumably, took care of the question of how Morton felt.

Another wire was from all the other Republican congressmen from Indiana, begging him to accept because "the interest of the country demands it."

But perhaps it was the message of Ben's Civil War comrades that really made up his mind for him. It said simply: "You can save the state." In the face of such faith, he knew he could not decline to try.

The moment his affirmative decision was known, of course, he became the target of the Democrats, particularly of the political cartoonists. What a contrast he—five-foot-six, sprucely dressed, with neatly trimmed beard and a penchant for wearing kid gloves—made with the six-foot-four, ungainly, overall-covered, and carefully not-too-clean Jimmy Williams!

Ben, in typical fashion, undertook to study the important political issues of the campaign. Foremost among them was the matter of hard versus soft money (gold or silver coin versus greenbacks or paper currency).

During the Civil War the trade of the country had been carried on largely through the medium of depreciated paper currency—bills that didn't have a definite amount of metal money backing them. After the war, business and financial leaders wanted to make such money illegal and to issue instead "legal tender notes" that could be redeemed at face value: a dollar's worth of gold, for example, for a dollar bill labeled a "gold certificate."

Those who wanted "cheap" money were called "inflationists." Rutherford Hayes, the Republican nominee for President, was a "sound money" man, or anti-inflationist.

Benjamin Harrison, after studying the pros and cons of the money issue, decided that he was anti-inflationist too, and he must try to convince the voters of Indiana why *they* should be.

He was sure they did not really understand the problem, so he used the simplest illustration possible:

"Imagine you have two pieces of pasteboard. One says, 'Good for one pint of milk.' The other says, 'This is a pint of milk.' Which do you think would get you the liquid you want to stir into your coffee?"

He sought, of course, to show the people that if they wanted to be sure of getting a pint of milk when they expected a pint of milk, they had to vote for the Republicans. By implication, then, he was saying that, with the Democrats in power, they might get half a pint instead.

Harrison believed every word he said, and his Republican audiences believed it too. However, he was up against not only a Democratic Party opponent but also, as it turned out, the candidate of the new Independent, or Greenback, Party, agitating vigorously for "paper money and lots of it." It drew its adherents from dissatisfied voters of both major parties.

The state election was held on Tuesday, October 10. For two days the outcome was in doubt, but in the end "Blue Jeans" Williams won by a small majority.

Ben was, naturally, disappointed, but he could not fault himself. He had fought a good fight, and he knew it. So did Indiana stalwarts of his party, and they thanked him and congratulated him for his splendid showing when he had entered the race so late.

He had, in fact, so nearly won that he was clearly considered a leader—if not *the* leader—now in Indiana party politics. In recognition of this status, he was asked to campaign actively for the national ticket, specifically in the doubtful states of New Jersey and Pennsylvania.

Both received him cordially, and he won a great many friends and admirers who were to remain steadfast throughout the rest of his life.

All in all, Harrison spent two weeks in extensive travel and speech-making. He came to identify so with the nominee from Ohio that he would feel a Hayes defeat or victory as if it were his own.

The outcome of the presidential election of 1876 was in doubt a far longer time than the Indiana state election had been. An electoral commission had to be appointed to decide upon disputed returns, but finally Hayes was declared the winner.

Hayes was not unaware of Harrison's efforts on his behalf. Indeed, the President-elect seriously considered appointing Ben as Secretary of the Navy in his Cabinet. He was deterred because of the powerful Oliver Morton's known opposition to or jealousy of his fellow Hoosier. Once again, Morton's choice took precedence. Instead of Harrison, Richard Wigginton Thompson received the appointment.

It had taken ten years, but now at last Ben had to admit that his former friend was now his enemy, at least in political matters. So be it. He would no longer defer to the older man. He would try to steer Indiana politics where *he* wanted them to go.

Fortunately, he had another contact besides Morton in Washington. Ironically, that was Richard Thompson. Morton surely could not have known it, when he chose Thompson over Harrison, but Thompson had been an intimate friend of Ben's since Civil War days.

CHAPTER **10**

Party Leader

THE YEAR 1877 was marked by labor unrest. Throughout
the country working men were complaining about their
treatment by management, about being overworked and
underpaid. Many wanted to do something drastic about it,
but most shrank at the idea of starting an actual revolt.
Finally, in June, workers on the Baltimore and Ohio Railroad were told they would have to take another ten percent cut in wages—the second since 1873—and their pa-
tience snapped. They refused to work and so effectively
halted the trains for which they were responsible. Railroad
workers on other lines soon followed suit, until almost all
traffic in Maryland, Pennsylvania, Ohio, and Indiana was at
a standstill.

In Indianapolis on July 24, strikers took possession of
the Union Depot. Afraid that his city would suffer rioting
and vandalism such as Pittsburgh had endured, the mayor
called on all law-abiding citizens to meet en masse in front
of the new courthouse at 7:30 P.M., adding that "measures
for organization for the protection of life and property will
be adopted."

The meeting was well attended and party lines were forgotten as men banded together to fight a common peril. A
Committee of Public Safety was appointed. So was a Committee of Mediation. Benjamin Harrison was chosen as
spokesman of the latter, empowered to deal directly with
the strikers.

The Committee on Safety called on the "volunteer militia" of some two hundred men to stand by for emergency action. Harrison was appalled at the idea of neighbor shooting at neighbor. He begged that the Committee on Mediation be allowed a real chance at solving the dilemma peacefully before the militia made a move.

He spoke quietly but firmly to a strikers' committee. He agreed that their wages were too low, and he promised to use his influence and that of the committee to get an increase. But in the meantime, he urged, the laborers should return to work.

"Citizens will not long tolerate mob rule," he warned, and told of the presence of the militia. "The sooner you realize that you are breaking the laws of the land, the sooner you will regain the sympathy and the confidence of the public and gain your ends."

Harrison's appeal to reason had its desired effect. The strike ended.

Ben's success was noted with favor by his fellow Hoosiers, and soon talk began about running him for senator in opposition to Senator Morton. Ben didn't commit himself as to how he felt about such a contest, and subsequent events made him grateful that he had not. Senator Morton was taken sick early in August, 1877, and died in November.

Eight months later, in May, 1878, another death occurred that brought far more personal grief to Ben—that of his father, John Harrison. Ben and Carrie went to North Bend at once and stayed for the sad event of the funeral. But shortly afterwards Ben had to return to Indianapolis. He was scheduled to give the keynote address at the state convention on June 5. He knew his father would have been the first to tell him he must forget self for country.

It was his first appearance as undisputed state leader, and he was received enthusiastically. He used the occasion to underscore Republican beliefs, particularly the sound money doctrine. In Washington, President Hayes was struggling with the same issue against a largely hostile Congress.

The fear of specie payment—redeeming of greenbacks at national dollar value—had been one of the powerful influences against the Republicans in the campaign of 1876. The Greenback, or cheap money, movement had defeated the state ticket then. It threatened to be an even greater problem in 1878, as specie payments were scheduled by law to be made as of January 1, 1879.

In his gubernatorial campaign of 1876, Ben had harped on the necessity for having a sound currency: "Those who buy and those who sell and those who work ought to know when they contract what the dollar of payment is to be." He planned to stump the state in 1878 repeating the same refrain, and that's what he did. But once again the Greenback movement was too strong. Election day, 1878, saw the Republicans go down to defeat in the state again, and indeed country-wide.

All the Democrat and Greenback insistence that resumption of specie payments would ruin the country proved as false as Hayes and Harrison had hoped it would. On Resumption Day, January 1, 1879, Hayes's Secretary of the Treasury, John Sherman, had more than enough gold to redeem all greenbacks that were turned in. This evidence that they *could* get dollar-for-dollar value satisfied the people, and public confidence in the national treasury was restored.

Confidence in the Republican Party was restored at the same time, and President Hayes was now praised for his intelligent farsightedness instead of being criticized for his pigheadedness.

Hoosiers recognized that Harrison, like Hayes, had known what he was talking about, too, and his personal political stock rose accordingly. He was not running for any political office just then, but he took advantage of his improved position to influence voters.

The country now faced another presidential election. Hayes had declared he would not run for re-election, and Grant let it be known that he would be "willing" to do so. This Harrison could not approve. However personally blameless of wrongdoing Grant might have been, his administration had been highly corrupt. Hayes had labored against enormous odds and brought the Republican Party back into favor. Should all his sacrifice be in vain? Not if Benjamin Harrison could help it!

All Harrison's speeches prior to the Republican National Convention of 1880 were directed to his point, and he went to Chicago on June 2 leading an Indiana delegation that was like himself opposed to Grant. James G. Blaine was the man they favored, though they were agreed that they would back partisan choice of any good man who could unite the party.

The Hoosier delegates tipped their hand on the first ballot by voting strongly for Blaine. They kept faithful to him through ballot after ballot, a service that Blaine obviously appreciated. By the thirty-fourth ballot, General James A. Garfield became a serious contender. At the same time Blaine lost strength, and it became obvious he could not win. Since Garfield was acceptable to Harrison and his Hoosiers, they jumped on his bandwagon. With the thirty-sixth ballot, Garfield won the nomination.

Harrison was given the honor of making the final speech urging that Garfield's nomination be declared unanimous. He made it very short, concluding: "I will defer my speech until the campaign is hot, and then, on every stump in Indiana, and *wherever else* my voice can help this great Republican cause on to victory, I hope to be found."

Harrison had not only Garfield and the national ticket to stump for but also the state ticket. His former partner, Albert Porter, was running for governor, and of course that gave added impetus to Ben's oratory.

The Democrats had very little ammunition to fire this year, because most issues had been settled during the Hayes years. As a result, they dug deep trying to find mud to sling. Ben was particularly distressed when Thomas Hendricks, the Democratic vice-presidential candidate who had run with Tilden against Hayes and Wheeler, accused Garfield of helping to steal the Presidency in 1876 from the Democrats.

Hendricks based his attack on the fact that Garfield had been part of the delegation sent to Louisiana to watch the recount of suspected votes. Harrison, eager to prove Hendricks wrong, wired Garfield to send proof that the count had been fair. Garfield complied, and Harrison told Hendricks off. According to a press report of the time, Harrison showed Hendricks up as "a garbler of testimony, a misrepresenter of the truth of history, and a public calumniator of private character."

Naturally, Garfield was grateful to Harrison for this service, and he wrote to tell Ben he hoped he could "reciprocate in kind" someday. Moreover, from that time forward Garfield considered Harrison a close friend and esteemed advisor.

The state elections in October, 1880, resulted in a grand victory for the Republican Party, and this was looked on as a good omen for national success in November. National leaders, aware of the importance of Harrison's part in this Hoosier showing, urged Ben to "travel abroad"—that is, away from Indiana—to continue his good work.

At first Ben hesitated. His law practice needed personal attention, and so did his family. However, he remembered his promise to speak "anywhere my voice can help the great Republican cause," and so he consented.

Garfield was elected with votes to spare. Afterward, Harrison sat down and wrote the new President a personal note of congratulation. In that letter, Harrison confessed to Garfield that he had decided to try for national office himself—for the vacant United States Senate seat.

Perhaps by making his announcement he wished subtly to inform Garfield he might need Garfield's backing. Perhaps he hoped to prevent a grateful Garfield from offering him the Cabinet post he might have had he not known of Harrison's desires. Whatever Harrison's reason, Garfield was noncommittal in his reply. He simply thanked Ben and said he hoped to see both General and Mrs. Harrison at his Ohio home before long.

Shortly after that correspondence, Ben formally announced his candidacy for the Senate, and his subsequent actions showed that he was going to pull out all the stops to insure his election. He sent letters to key Republicans in all parts of the state, reminding them that he was a straight party man, meaning that he favored sound money and a high protective tariff. He added that soldiers might expect "appreciative recognition" from him, and the laboring man "a fair and honest hearing."

The Indianapolis legislature convened on January 6, 1881, and on the eleventh, Benjamin Harrison's name was presented to the Republican senatorial caucus. The nomination was quickly seconded and almost as quickly made fact by unanimous vote. On the eighteenth, the legislature duly elected him.

At once congratulations poured in from all over the country, from people high up in national politics, from former classmates, from members of his regiment, and of course from family and friends. President Hayes wrote him most cordially. But from the President-elect there was at first no word.

This omission worried Ben a little. Would Garfield take Ben's election with good grace and choose another man from Indiana to fill the Cabinet post he'd set aside as a political plum for that state?

When Garfield finally did write, he asked Ben to come to Mentor, his Ohio home, for a "quiet little talk." Ben agreed, and on arriving there quickly made it clear to Garfield that he felt he could serve the party better in the Senate than in a Cabinet berth.

He also tried to convince Garfield that some other Hoosier—and he named several men—would be well suited to the Cabinet post, but his efforts were in vain.

"I do not see that I can make a selection from Indiana for the Cabinet unless it be you," Garfield said.

It was hard for Ben to stick to his resolution in the face of such pressure, but he did. He went to Washington as senator in February, 1881. With him went his wife and his twenty-two-year-old daughter, Mamie. His son, Russell, joined them on March 4, Inauguration Day.

On March 5, Harrison began his senatorial career at the first special session of the Forty-seventh Congress. The special session was called to consider the Cabinet appointments of the new President. All were confirmed without question, but that was the only time for weeks that the senators agreed easily on anything. Their "dog-fighting and back-biting" as they fought for control of key committees distressed Ben, as did the constant maneuvering for favors that he witnessed among his colleagues.

Being a very new senator, Ben only watched during his first session. He was appointed to four committees: Indian affairs, the military, territories, and rules. But none of them met before the special session adjourned on May 20.

Ben had hoped to travel to the western territories so that he would have firsthand knowledge of them to help in his coming committee work. However, once back in Indianapolis he had first to pay a little attention to legal clients. While he was still attending to their business, he heard the shocking news that President Garfield had been shot and might not recover.

That was on July 2. Harrison went immediately to Washington, where he stayed until he was convinced that Garfield was actually on the mend. Then he returned to Indianapolis and, as soon as he could, did go on the western trip. He spent some extra time in the territory of Montana, where his son Russell was in the cattle business.

He was in Chicago on September 20 when news of Garfield's death reached him. He returned once more to Washington, to attend the state funeral. Then he accompanied Mrs. Garfield—"the most heroic woman I have ever known"—back to Ohio for the final burial of his friend.

Chester A. Arthur was now the President, to nearly everyone's consternation. Arthur had no qualifications for the office, his sole political position previously having been collector of the Port of New York. President Grant had appointed him, but he proved so corrupt, so eager to accept bribes, that President Hayes had removed him from that office.

To everyone's surprise, however, Arthur showed every evidence of having reformed. He refused to use his position to reward his former cronies. Moreover, in his first message to Congress he indicated his willingness to cooperate with the legislators in breaking up the practice of giving jobs as rewards.

The Forty-seventh Congress reconvened on December 6, 1881. Harrison quickly found out that the real business of the nation was conducted in the committee rooms. He strove to make his presence felt there, in each of the committees to which he belonged.

The first measure of real importance in which Ben took a prominent part was that relating to the suspension of Chinese immigration. The story behind the measure was this. In the late 1860's, Pacific coast men encouraged Chinese laborers to come to the United States to work on the construction of railroads. In 1868, Anson Burlingame, United States minister to China, negotiated a treaty with China, permitting unrestricted immigration as well as promising equality of treatment with immigrants of other countries. However, shortly after 1870 it became apparent that the Chinese, in competing with American laborers, were in fact endangering American standards by virtue of their own low economic standards. In 1879, Congress tried to repeal the treaty, but President Hayes vetoed the repeal. Instead, he sent a commission to China to modify the treaty. The new treaty went into effect in November, 1880. It gave the United States government the right to "regulate, limit or suspend" the entry of Chinese laborers into the United States, although it could not "prohibit." It further said that the limitation or suspension should be "reasonable."

The Forty-seventh Congress took the view that the treaty terms were ambiguous and in the spring of 1882 indulged in prolonged debate over just what they did mean. Finally, the Congress passed a bill that *would* prohibit Chinese immigration, for a period of twenty years.

At the time of the Chinese Exclusion Bill's passage, Harrison was absent from the Senate on committee business and therefore did not get a chance to vote. He heard about the bill immediately, of course, and objected. It wasn't that he did not approve the restriction of Chinese labor—he did— but he believed that Congress had no right to override the treaty.

"A treaty is, in its nature, a contract between two nations, not a legislative act," he insisted.

This stand was contrary to the Republican Party's views, and Ben's colleagues criticized him roundly for his independent position.

President Arthur vetoed the bill, so it returned to Congress. This time, Ben was there to present his objections loudly and vigorously. He made the point that the bill was "Un-American," that it "repudiated the spirit of the Constitution."

His words had not enough effect on his colleagues. The bill passed both houses of Congress with only slight modification, and this time President Arthur did not veto it.

Another issue that had the attention of the Forty-seventh Congress in its first regular session was the matter of the tariff. "Protective tariff and encouragement of American industry" had been one of William Henry Harrison's campaign slogans in 1840, so it had been natural for his grandson to be interested in the tariff regulations since the nation's beginnings.

The Tariff Act of 1789 had been largely for revenue, as had the Tariff of 1812. In 1816, the first tariff really protective to American industry had been passed, putting high duties on the importation of cotton, wool, and iron. In 1846 the trend was again reversed, the tariff being largely a revenue collection and so letting some formerly taxed items into the country free. The Tariff of 1857 was similar, except that it allowed for many more free imports. The Tariff of 1861 had raised duties again—and so things had gone in see-saw fashion through the years.

In 1882 the country was working under tariff regulations that were again highly protective, and the Democrats did not like them. Since it was a time of surplus in the national treasury, they claimed that the tariff should again be reduced. As it stood, it was hurting, not helping, American industry, they claimed. In their party platform they had taken a stand for "revision of the present unjust tariff."

The other senator from Indiana was a Democrat, Daniel Voorhees, and he was as rabid on the subject as anybody. Harrison could not understand why, since Indiana wasn't "hurting." On the contrary, Indiana agriculture and industry were both thriving, or had been the last time he'd looked into the matter. However, he did realize that he was in no position to challenge Voorhees on the Senate floor. He had not had time really to study the situation, and conditions of industry and trade did change constantly. Therefore, he gladly backed the congressional move which authorized the President to appoint a nine-man commission to study the situation and make recommendations.

The Republican Party had, since its beginning, stood for a high protective tariff. Not surprisingly, therefore, the Republican President Arthur packed the commission with protectionists. Its chairman, in fact, was secretary of the National Association of Wool Manufacturers. What was surprising was the commission's recommendation: a general reduction in duties to the 20 percent level (in 1867 they had been at 47 percent).

President Arthur passed the recommendation on to the Congress. Having previously given implied consent to abide by the commission's decision, the legislators undertook to pass the necessary legislation. But what a stir arose! Lobbyists from all over the country swarmed into Washington to plead for their special interests.

Benjamin Harrison was among those beset with pressure from home. The manufacture of jute (burlap) bags was big business in Indiana. If the duty on the import of such bags from East India were reduced any further, Indiana baggers would have to close up shop. Similarly, glass manufacturers objected to reduction in the import duty on foreign glass.

The result was that Congress backed away from its original plan. It passed what was later derisively called the Mongrel Tariff of 1883, which did little to change matters. The surplus would not only remain in the treasury as a temptation to legislators to back pet schemes for their constituents, but it would increase.

Soon after the passage of the Mongrel Bill, Congress adjourned. Harrison and his family returned to Indianapolis, where Ben found it necessary to mend some political fences. He was still being criticized for patronage appointments he had made, particularly his selection of postmasters. He had tried to select them according to merit, but he had been forced to rely often upon suggestions of friends. Many of the appointments had turned out to be unwise, and as a result people were complaining.

Ben did not blame them, and he was happy to be able to say that "soon such jobs will be given only to people who have passed competitive examinations."

This was an optimistic statement, sparked by the recent passage of the civil service law of 1883. Known as the Pendleton Act, it authorized the President to appoint three civil service commissioners with power to conduct competitive examinations for officeholders in branches of the public service that were "classified" by the President or Congress. So far, however, only a few offices were classified, and so only about one-tenth of the total number of federal employees was affected.

Ben was undoubtedly unhappy at being unpopular with the people of his home state. He was certainly upset by evidences that he was also losing political prestige. Most flagrant of these was President Arthur's choice of Indiana's Judge Walter Q. Gresham as his Postmaster General. Gresham and Harrison had a history of disagreeing with each other in court, for their standards were incompatible. President Arthur was aware of this. Therefore, by appointing Gresham to his Cabinet, he was as good as "slapping Harrison in the face." It was a bitter pill for Ben to swallow.

Ben's popularity in Indiana was less than he would have liked, but outside his home state he was in demand as a stump speaker in the off-year elections. He gave many talks in Iowa and Ohio, each time gaining more and more admirers. He explained the tariff and the civil service enactments so that everybody could understand what they meant for the country. Said the *Iowa State Register* in September, 1883: "His ready conversance with public affairs, and with the details of government, and his remarkable use of such knowledge, prove his mastery both in statement and argument."

The off-year elections gave back to the Republicans four of the seats they had lost in the Democratic resurgence of 1882, and the national party credited Ben with helping accomplish this. Consequently, when he returned to Washington for the Forty-eighth Congress, he was again held in esteem.

From that time forward, he devoted himself to legislation that particularly interested him, and he was able to push through a bill for the relief of disabled soldiers and their widows. This pleased G.A.R. organizations, and they were loud in their praise for "Little Ben, the Soldiers' Friend."

Harrison's work on the committee concerned with territories was also notable, particularly his efforts on behalf of statehood for South Dakota. He used all his oratorical powers, and used them convincingly. He gave facts and figures to show that the southern portion of Dakota Territory had a population of over 300,000, and that its total produce far exceeded Nevada's and Colorado's combined.

He was able to convince the committee and got a bill introduced into the Senate. Here it ran into trouble, because

the Senate was largely Democratic, and the territory largely
Republican. One delay after another beset it, until Harrison must have despaired of its ever getting past the discussion stage. Finally, just before Christmas recess, 1884, it
went to a vote and was passed by a narrow margin.

Ben could not feel it was a victory, though, because he
knew the delay had been deliberate. The House of Representatives would not now have time to act. And after
Christmas the legislators would be too taken up with the
inauguration of a new President to pay attention to such
an unpopular measure.

The presidential campaign of 1884 had been the most
abusive one in the country's history so far. The Republican
nominee was James G. Blaine; the Democratic, Grover
Cleveland. Each side accused the other of corrupt dealings
and dug deep to prove immorality as well.

Harrison, of course, was a friend of Blaine's and had
backed him through more than thirty ballots in the convention that finally nominated Garfield. Naturally, Blaine
had hoped that Harrison could deliver Indiana to him in
the November, 1884, election. However, the Democrats
had made this nearly impossible the moment they chose
Indiana's Thomas Hendricks as the vice-presidential candidate.

The friendship Harrison felt for Blaine did make him
feel obliged to agree to represent Blaine in a suit against the
Democratic Indianapolis *Sentinel*, protesting a morals attack. Ben first had to be convinced that the charges were
false, and by the time he was ready to go into court to
vindicate his friend, Blaine changed his mind. He said he
had decided it would be unwise to air the issue any more
before election.

This withdrawal was embarrassing to Harrison, who had
advised the *Sentinel* of the impending suit, reserved court

time, and so on. Moreover, it proved damaging four years later, when political enemies alleged that Ben had refused to go to court in the hope that he could eliminate Blaine as competition in 1888.

The dirtiest campaign ever finally ended, and Grover Cleveland was declared the winner by a very close vote. Indiana had gone for Cleveland, however, and though Ben had expected this, he was disappointed.

The Democrats swept into state offices too, and this was to have important repercussions on Ben's senatorial future. They decided to gerrymander—that is, redistrict—the state, to set it up in such a way as to secure the future advantage of their own party.

Harrison saw at once what passage of such an unfair measure would mean to him. He called it "A Bill to Prohibit the Election of a Republican Senator in Indiana."

The bill passed, and in 1886 Harrison was its prize victim. He lost his bid for re-election to the Senate.

CHAPTER 11

The Whole Show

ON MARCH 3, 1887, Ben yielded his Senate seat to his successor, David Turpie. Shortly after that, he and Carrie returned to Indianapolis.

At first Ben felt let down at suddenly being a private citizen again. Within a few days, however, he had something to rejoice about. His daughter Mamie—since November, 1884, Mrs. Robert McKee—made him a grandfather. She named the baby after him: Benjamin Harrison McKee. He became known at once as Baby McKee, the nickname which was to follow him a good many years of his life.

The baby's birth seemed to give Harrison a new lease on life. He plunged back into his law practice with vigor and soon was flooded with important cases. He managed to keep busy and happy until time for vacation rolled around in August. Then he took his family—Carrie and the McKees— off to Deer Park, Maryland, where his friend Henry Davis, an ex-senator from West Virginia, had placed a cottage at his disposal.

The cottage next door, also owned by Davis, was occupied by Davis and his daughter and son-in-law, the Stephen Elkinses. The neighbors spent a good deal of time together, and inevitably talk turned to politics.

Elkins had supported Blaine in 1884, and he thought that Blaine wanted to run again. Davis, however, said that Republicans needed a citizen-soldier if they hoped to beat Cleveland in 1888.

"You yourself are presidential timber," Davis said to Harrison.

Ben was flattered, but he was also realistic. If Blaine wanted the nomination, he would get it. He, Harrison, would certainly not try to oppose the "Man from Maine" himself.

But in October, 1887, word came from Blaine, who was touring Europe. "I feel very strongly disinclined to run . . . I do not want the turmoil and burdensome exactions of a canvass . . . above all, I abhor the idea of becoming a chronic candidate."

"Disinclined" did not necessarily mean that he *declined*, although some Republicans were ready to take that as Blaine's meaning. Harrison himself favored a wait and see attitude. Either Blaine wanted to be the party leader or he didn't. He would have to show his hand before too long.

President Cleveland forced Blaine to do so. For months Cleveland had fought with Congress to really reduce tariff duties. The Mongrel Tariff, he told legislators, had not really done any good. The surplus in the treasury was still enormous. Besides, the high protective tariff was "a ruthless extortion of the people's money and a violation of the fundamental principles of free government," he said.

Congress kept ignoring his wishes, so he decided to take his case to the people. Knowing that the newspapers would report fully what he said, he devoted his entire Annual Message, delivered December 6, 1887, to a plea for a lowered protective tariff. He pointed out that the existing rates had encouraged the creation of trusts and the maintenance of high prices, that the people were in effect being robbed by big business.

Harrison read Cleveland's message and knew its importance. A high protective tariff was part of basic Republican doctrine. If Blaine truly wanted to carry the party's banner, he would have to reply to Cleveland without delay.

Within two days, Blaine's answer came from Paris. It, like Cleveland's message, was printed in every important paper in the United States. Said a commentator of that reply:

"In twenty lines . . . Blaine managed to appeal to high protectionists, lovers of cheap tobacco, haters of England, temperance advocates, coast-defense enthusiasts, and those who thought Cleveland was a poor Democrat compared to Tilden."

Republicans all over the country accepted Blaine's "straight from the shoulder" rejoinder as evidence that the Man from Maine did want to be counted in as a candidate. Benjamin Harrison considered that its meaning, too, and so did Theodore Roosevelt, Henry Cabot Lodge, and John Hay. All of them cabled Blaine their congratulations, promising to back him to the limit.

But they were all mistaken. On January 25, 1888, Blaine wrote a letter to the Chairman of the Republican National Committee. In it he said he would not *under any circumstances* be a candidate for the Presidency in 1888. Now at last Blaine's supporters had to accept the fact that they must look elsewhere for a standard-bearer.

Blaine's withdrawal gave hope to any number of prominent men who would not have considered opposing him. Among them were William B. Allison of Iowa and John Sherman of Ohio, both of whom had gained national importance during the Hayes administration. Allison and Sherman began to agitate forcefully, and their deeds and ideas received daily coverage in the nation's newspapers.

Benjamin Harrison, however, for a time did nothing overt at all. This seeming indifference puzzled and irritated his friends, particularly Davis and Elkins. At Deer Park the previous summer they had told him he could "inherit the Blaine mantle" if Blaine took himself out of the picture. Well, Blaine was out now.

Ben was not indifferent, but he was wary. He knew that the announced candidates were far better known nationally than he, and he did not want to run in a race that he had not a fair chance of winning.

Friends who knew Ben better than Elkins and Davis soon recognized his diffidence for what it was. They began to work behind the scenes to build his image. When they were fairly sure he really was the man most favored by a majority of top party regulars, they reported the fact to Ben.

The time had come to toss his hat into the ring, if he was going to, and Ben knew it. Now he waited only for what he considered favorable circumstances in which to do it.

An invitation to speak at a Washington's birthday banquet in Detroit provided the perfect occasion. Held in the Michigan Club, considered the most influential organization in the state, the dinner was attended by Republican Party leaders from all the midwestern states and even from a few of the eastern block.

In his address to this powerful audience, Harrison was careful to speak of national issues in terms of their importance to local interests. He therefore easily won his listeners' attention and approval. The Detroit newspapers fully reported the text of the speech and the guests' reaction to it. Indiana papers joyfully spread the word of "our Ben's success," and the nation's press soon followed suit.

Once having declared himself a candidate, Harrison proceeded to toot his own horn—but softly. He realized that the high protective tariff would have to be the chief plank in the Republican platform. Cleveland's advocacy of tariff reform indicating what stand he would face as the Democratic candidate had driven the first nail into it. But Ben

chose to speak of that issue metaphorically, using the image
of the ship of state to indicate the national government.
His speech of March 20, 1888, before a Young Republican's
Club in Chicago, illustrated this most colorfully. It also
served to wave the bloody shirt discreetly, thereby reminding people which party was to blame for the Civil War.

> We took the ship of state when there was treachery at the helm . . .
> we brought the deck into order and subjection . . . we have brought
> the ship into the sea of prosperity. Is it to be suggested that the party
> that has accomplished those magnificent achievements cannot sail and
> manage that ship in the frequented roadways of ordinary commerce?

This speech won influential independent Republicans
over to Harrison's side. They remembered his excellent
record as a soldier and his clean, if undistinguished, record
as a senator. Union veterans, too, were solidly behind Little
Ben, so by mid-April it did look as if Harrison had an above-
average chance of being his party's presidential nominee.

Harrison was cheered by the statistics of voter strength
that were shown him, but he was made uneasy by rumors
that Blaine would still accept a draft.

"The battle isn't over till the last gun is fired," he said,
knowing from experience that that was true.

The Republican National Convention opened in Chicago on June 19, 1888. The Indiana delegation went there
pledged solidly for Harrison. Ben himself stayed home,
ostensibly to attend to the press of business.

The men who called themselves the Harrison Committee
had set up headquarters in Chicago a full week before the
Convention. They had been working to see that Harrison
boosters were represented in every Convention committee.
They particularly wanted to insure the drafting of a party
platform on which Harrison could stand comfortably. They
knew the Presbyterian integrity of their candidate.

All this was necessary, because even without Blaine there

were still formidable competitors with Harrison. Neither John Sherman nor William Allison had bowed out.

The men of the Harrison Committee were somewhat hampered by Ben's solemn warning to them: Make no promises for me. Wheeling and dealing was part of the political game, and would-be kingmakers were expected to play it properly.

This fact was clearly brought home to them when Pennsylvania's "boss," Matthew Quay, indicated that he was willing to leave John Sherman for Harrison *if* he could be assured his state would thereby receive a Cabinet post. The Harrison men knew that Pennsylvania's votes might make all the difference to a candidate's chances, but they didn't dare go counter to Harrison's wishes. Therefore, they composed a letter that promised Quay what he wanted and sent it to Ben accompanied by the hopeful request that he sign it.

He would not. He repeated what he had said before:

"I may want to be President, but if I am to go to the White House, I don't propose to go shackled."

The first two days of the Convention itself were taken up with routine duties of delegate seating and partisan pep talks. On the third day William McKinley of Ohio read the report of the platform committee. It brought joy to Harrison men, because there was nothing in it that could embarrass Harrison in the event of his nomination.

At noon on June 21 the alphabetical roll call of the states began. Various states called before Indiana proposed favorite son candidates. Then Indiana's turn came, and Ben's former partner, Governor Albert Porter, presented his name.

Porter pulled out all the stops. He reminded the Convention of Ben's illustrious ancestors, Benjamin the Declaration signer and Old Tippecanoe. He recalled Ben's military achievements, his blameless congressional record. He concluded, "No other name is so woven into the fabric of American history as that of Harrison," and sat down to a roar of applause.

Balloting began on June 22 at 11:05 A.M. California startled everyone by casting all its votes for Blaine, whose name had not even been introduced. What did it mean? Would, as the Sherman men feared aloud, "the Blaine lunatics" stampede the Convention?

They didn't, but the spread of votes among other candidates was large. Out of 831 votes cast, with 416 necessary to elect, Harrison came in fourth, behind Sherman, Walter Q. Gresham of Ohio, and Chauncey Depew of New York.

Two more ballots showed gains for all but Depew, and apparently the trend discouraged New York's choice. He decided to withdraw and release his delegation, led by "Boss" Thomas Platt. Even so, the next two ballots were indecisive, and then the Convention adjourned for the weekend. The time for real bargaining had come, if there was to be any.

On Sunday, word came from Blaine to Elkins, who had always been first for him, second for Harrison. Blaine was firm in his refusal to be considered and asked that his name be withdrawn at once. "Harrison should be the one," he directed.

At once, Elkins went to see Boss Platt. What was said no one ever knew, but when balloting began again on Monday morning, New York went solidly for Harrison.

Early on that same morning back in Indianapolis, Harrison had pushed through a group of excited townspeople to reach his law office. There his partner, William Henry Harrison Miller, and several friends were waiting for him. Nearby was a rented telegraphic instrument, installed to give them the news from Chicago quickly.

After the sixth ballot the word of New York's capitulation flashed over the wires. When the seventh ballot showed California, too, leaving Blaine for Harrison, the listeners in Indianapolis could scarcely restrain themselves.

"What do you think?" one of them asked Ben.

"I feel much more disturbed now than I did when I thought sure it would be defeat," he answered. "There is too much seriousness about such a position to take it in stride."

On the eighth ballot Harrison's victory was assured, for he got 128 votes more than necessary. At once, the streets of Indianapolis were full of laughing, shouting, snake-dancing people, of marching bands and waving flags. Hundreds of men and women crowded up the stairs and into Harrison's office. Everybody wanted to shake his hand.

As soon as he decently could, Ben headed for home to give Carrie the news. It had arrived there before him, however, and souvenir seekers were already taking apart the white picket fence surrounding the yard. When they saw Harrison, they sent up a rousing cheer, but they were not diverted from their purpose.

That evening Ben gave the first of what were to be many informal front porch talks, for in the next few weeks thousands of well-wishers came to Indianapolis to pay tribute to Harrison. Among the groups to arrive en masse were the complete delegations from California and New York. Ben was aware how large a part those delegations had played in his nomination, and he thanked them for their services. He did not know that, or even *if*, any deals had been made to gain their support, but just in case, he made his own point of view crystal clear.

"I feel sure, my fellow citizens, that we have joined now a contest of great principles, and that the armies which are to fight . . . will encamp upon the high plains of those principles, and not in the low swamps of personal defamation and detraction."

According to custom, a committee of one man from each state had been appointed to make formal announcement to Harrison and his vice-presidential running mate, Levi P. Morton of New York, of their nomination. The committee chose July 4 as the day to call upon Ben in his Indianapolis home, and he was pleased by the appropriateness of the date. He spoke of it in his reply to their announcement.

"The day you have chosen for this visit suggests no thoughts not in harmony with the occasion. The Republican Party has walked in the light of the Declaration of Independence. It has lifted the shaft of patriotism upon the foundation laid at Bunker Hill. It has made the more perfect Union secure by making all men free."

Now that Benjamin Harrison was a national figure, everything about him was interesting to the country. It was up to his promoters to make him seem everything the American public admired or needed. Whenever possible, they managed the news, stressing the details most calculated to please potential voters.

Among the homey details were glimpses of Harrison's home life: his delight in playing with Baby McKee, his pride in his wife's delicate watercolor paintings, his pleasure in cultivating grapevines, his willingness to chitchat over the back fence with neighbors. Not forgotten either was his relationship to Old Tippecanoe or the many acts of kindness he had extended to his regiment during the war.

Ben realized that all this personal publicity was necessary to combat the charges that he was rich and snobbish and cold, but he did not approve of it. He would very much have preferred having his private and public life kept completely separate.

The front porch talks Ben had given soon after the con-

vention proved to be so good for his public image that his
campaign counselors suggested he resume them. He did, and
between mid-July and mid-October he delivered more than
eighty informal speeches in this fashion. He spoke to crowds
ranging from fifty to fifty thousand, often giving three or
four speeches a day. So that they should be reported cor-
rectly to the nation's press, Harrison's private secretary,
Frank Tibbott, took them down in shorthand. He later
transcribed them for proofreading by Harrison, and only
after that was done were they sent out over Associated Press
wires.

In all his speeches Harrison stressed his love for America
first, last, and always. "We have men who boast that they are
cosmopolitan, citizens of the world. I prefer to say that I am
an American citizen, and I freely confess that American
interests have first place in my regard."

When pressed to defend more clearly his stand on the
protective tariff, he said, "We should be slow to abandon
that system of protective duties which looks to the promotion of the highest scale of wages for the American working
man."

He did not forget the old bloody shirt issue, either, nor
the benefits he thought were due to the boys in blue who
had fought to preserve the Union. He reminded his coun-
trymen that, just because the nation was at peace, the
soldiers' sacrifices should not be forgotten.

"It is no time to use an apothecary's scale to weigh the rewards due the men who saved the country," he said.

At first the professional politicians—the party bosses—
had been afraid that Harrison might say something wrong
during his folksy off-the-cuff chats. As time went on, however, and he proved to be a master of tact, they realized that
they had no cause for worry. Even Boss Quay, the Chairman
of the Republican National Committee, finally agreed.

"Harrison himself is the whole show," he said. "If he has the strength to continue making those wonderful speeches to the end of the campaign, we can safely close headquarters and he can elect himself."

Quay did not close up headquarters, of course. He bent his persuasive powers to bringing in all financial help possible, so that Republicans could print and distribute tons of literature aimed at convincing voters of the advantages of the protective tariff over free trade. One of the largest financial contributors was John Wanamaker, Philadelphia's department store king.

Harrison's friends did worry about how his health would stand up under the stress of delivering so many speeches. Finally, since he needed time to prepare his official acceptance letter, Ben agreed in mid-August to take a two-week vacation on an island in Lake Erie, out of reach of everybody.

President Cleveland's letter of acceptance was published first, on September 10. It was much like his December, 1887, Annual Message, really just a restatement of his free trade principles. Not surprisingly, it was received with indifference by the reading public.

Benjamin Harrison's acceptance letter was published two days later. Its content was largely concerned with standard Republican views on the protective tariff:

The Republican Party holds that a protective tariff is constitutional, wholesome, and necessary. We do not offer a fixed schedule, but a principle. We will revise the schedule, modify rates, but always with an intelligent prevision as to the effect upon domestic production and the wages of our working people. We believe . . . one of the worthy objects of tariff legislation is to *preserve the American market for American producers,* and to maintain the American scale of wages by putting adequate duties upon foreign competing products.

But it touched also on the importation of foreign laborers, election frauds, and civil service appointments. In short, every issue important to the American voter was clearly spoken to by the Republican candidate.

In contrast to the public disinterest accorded Cleveland's letter, Harrison's received both interest and praise. Hundreds of congratulatory letters and telegrams told Ben this, letters from little people as well as important ones. One telegram even said: "I wish I was as sure of going to heaven as I am that you will be elected."

The campaign, however, was not cut-and-dried by any means. Mud was thrown by both sides at each other's candidates, and not even Ben's own home state of Indiana could be considered surely in his camp. After all, President Cleveland had managed to carry the state by nearly 7,000 votes in the last election, and the current governor, himself a Democrat, boasted that he would deliver Indiana to Cleveland again.

This challenge finally convinced the Republican Committee it should send prize stump-speakers to help Ben on his home ground. Up till that point, they had felt he was doing very well by himself.

Although he was reluctant to admit it, Ben welcomed the thought of party help and asked specifically that Blaine be sent. Blaine had returned to the United States in August, and Ben felt his presence in Indiana could make all the difference.

Blaine arrived on October 11, 1888, and in his honor Indiana Republicans staged what the Associated Press said was quite possibly "the greatest political parade ever witnessed in the country"; 25,000 marchers passed in review before the hotel balcony where Blaine and the Harrisons stood and on to the Exposition grounds where Blaine was shortly scheduled to speak.

Blaine gave two speeches in Indianapolis, each blistering in its attack on Cleveland and his "inept" administration. During the following week he spoke many more places in Indiana and then went on to other key Midwest states. Everywhere he went he left his audiences hypnotized, conditioned to vote for Harrison or against Cleveland, the end result being the same.

The Republicans never let up. They fought in the press and on the platform. They mailed out over a million pieces of propaganda literature and an equal number of "documented denials" of every mud-slinging charge.

The climax of the campaign in Indiana had overtones of the William Henry Harrison campaign of 1840. A huge red and white canvas ball, measuring forty-two feet in circumference and fourteen in diameter, arrived in Indianapolis, having been rolled all the way from Cumberland, Maryland. Bigger than the campaign ball of 1840, this one contained even more slogans, printed in letters easy to read from a distance.

"Here it will remain until after election," said D. E. Brockett, the ball's custodian. "Then I will roll it on to Washington."

On election eve he rolled the ball up Delaware Street to Harrison's home. He was accompanied by hundreds of intrigued followers, all joining him in the song "We'll Keep the Ball A-Rolling On," which had been Ben's main memory of his grandfather's "Log Cabin and Hard Cider" campaign.

Ben, watching and applauding from the front stoop of his home, surely remembered and appreciated the parallel. He did not try to hide the fact that he was touched, for more than once he was seen to wipe tears from his eyes.

CHAPTER 12

Driving the Elephant

ON ELECTION DAY, after he returned home from casting his vote, Benjamin Harrison was handed a letter. It was from James Blaine, who well knew how the hours of such a day could drag. He wrote, "The day will be one of restlessness and I thought one more friendly assurance might agreeably engage your thoughts and your time for a few of the slowly moving minutes of that dragging period."

Luckily for Ben, he was kept company by his family, his law partners, and his closest friends and neighbors. They were there to rejoice with him when it became clear he had indeed won the election.

It was a bit sobering for Ben to know that, though winning by a large electoral count, he did lag behind Cleveland in the popular vote. But it was heartening to note that he had carried Indiana overwhelmingly.

Immediately following the election, while congratulations were still pouring in, President-elect Harrison was beset with suggestions as to whom he should pick for his Cabinet. He was also deluged with petitioners who wanted federal jobs. Ben reacted as he had during the campaign. He listened but kept his own counsel, acting only when and as he saw fit.

February 25, 1889, was announced as the day Harrison would depart for Washington. The president of the Pennsylvania Railroad offered him a private train for the trip.

An honor guard was set up to accompany him to the station. Thirty-two of the most prominent citizens of Indianapolis walked in a hollow square surrounding the Harrison carriage. Several columns of veterans marched before and behind. When the parade reached the State House, the members of the Indiana legislature joined the procession. And all along the route thousands of spectators waved their handkerchiefs, threw their hats into the air, and cheered lustily.

At the station, Harrison spoke movingly in farewell. Near the end of his little talk he said:

"There is a great sense of loneliness in the discharge of high public duties . . . but there is One to whose wise and unfailing guidance I shall look for direction and safety." He paused for a moment, then continued brokenly: "My family unite with me in grateful thanks for this cordial goodbye, and with me wish that these years of separation may be full of peace and happiness for each of you."

The progress of the train was slow. It stopped often to allow the people to see and hear the President-elect. He obliged by giving impromptu speeches from the rear platform.

His arrival in Washington was almost secret, however, for unbeknown to him, it had been arranged that the presidential party should detrain at the freight depot and be transported to the Johnson House annex of the Arlington Hotel.

Harrison had much to do, of course, before inauguration day. He previously had decided whom he wanted for his Cabinet and in fact had issued invitations secretly to most of his choices. He now must confer with them and read them his inaugural speech, as soon as he had finished polishing it. He must also, according to protocol, call on President Cleveland and be called upon in return.

In such pursuits he was kept very busy until March 4.
On that day he was awakened before dawn by the strains
of music played by arriving bands, and by the sound of
steadily falling rain as well. It was still raining at one
o'clock, when Harrison and Cleveland, arm in arm,
mounted the uncovered inaugural stand. All about them
was a sea of upraised umbrellas, but Harrison held his high
silk hat in his hand.

The court clerk held out an open Bible. Harrison solemnly placed his hand on it and, repeating the words after
Chief Justice Melville Fuller, took the oath that made him
the twenty-third President of the United States. Immediately afterward, Harrison put on his hat and drew his
speech from his pocket.

In that speech he strongly expressed his view of what the
President's role was.

I have altogether rejected the suggestion of a special executive
policy for any section of the country. It is the duty of the Executive to
administer and enforce, in the methods and by the instrumentalities
pointed out and provided by the Constitution, all the laws enacted by
Congress. These laws are general, and their administration should be
uniform and equal. . . . The evil example of permitting individuals,
corporations, or communities to nullify the laws because they cross
some selfish or local interests and prejudices, is full of danger.

He went on to speak of all key issues: the tariff, free ballot,
civil service laws, foreign affairs, naturalization legislation.
He asked God's help in dealing with them. In every word
he said, his consciousness of personal Christian responsibility was evident.

God has placed on our head a diadem, and has laid at our feet
power and wealth beyond definition or calculation. But we must not
forget that we take these gifts upon the condition that justice and
mercy shall hold the reins of power, and that the upward avenues of
hope shall be free to all the people.

The traditional White House luncheon followed the swearing-in and the speech. It in turn was followed by a parade, one that must have warmed Ben's patriotic heart in spite of the cold driving rain. For four hours, units of all the armed forces fast-marched by him, and then G.A.R. posts, in which he recognized many comrades from his war years. After them came marchers with placards, some of them picturing Ben proudly wearing his grandfather's hat (not the cartoon that had showed him bowed under the weight of it); the Cowboy Club of Denver, led by Buffalo Bill himself; firemen carrying red, white, and blue umbrellas; Negro marching clubs. Last of all rolled the big ball, now boasting the legend "Four, four, four years more," although the first year had just started.

Public announcement of President Harrison's Cabinet appointments predictably aroused some furor, particularly the choice of James G. Blaine as Secretary of State. Blaine's critics had warned Harrison earlier that Blaine would "either rule the administration or wreck it," and certainly Ben was not unaware of Blaine's strength. After all, he had come close to being President himself in 1884 and could easily have been the Republican nominee instead of Ben this time. But Ben was also aware of Blaine's weakness: love of self. He knew that putting Blaine in a key post was taking a calculated risk, but he thought the gamble was worthwhile. He said he believed Blaine capable of great public service *if* he would serve the administration first and himself second.

In his other Cabinet choices Ben had been independent of pressure also. His only criteria had been age and experience. Only two of the eight were younger than his own fifty-five years. Six were lawyers, two were businessmen. Each one was as devoted a churchgoer as Ben himself.

This was duly noted by the nation's press, which commented: "The Cabinet can be relied upon to help the

President keep the government as clean as possible," indicating that they thought Harrison's choices did him credit.

But they infuriated many power-mad party men who hadn't believed Harrison when he'd intimated that he intended to "drive the elephant alone." Why, it was their right to be bestowers of patronage and to be beneficiaries of it, too! Particularly incensed were the big city bosses, Quay of Philadelphia and Platt of New York. Platt, in fact, had wanted to be Secretary of the Treasury and felt personally slighted when Harrison had appointed the conservative Wall Street broker William Windom instead.

The Cabinet posts were not the only ones Harrison filled with people whom he felt were right for the job regardless of whose toes he was stepping on. He did the same in filling most offices over which he had the right of appointment.

One of these was the post of Civil Service Commissioner, which he offered to young Theodore Roosevelt. Roosevelt, then thirty, was an even more zealous foe of the spoils or patronage system than Ben himself. He accepted the position with alacrity. In later years, when he himself became President, he acknowledged his debt to Harrison.

"He gave me my first opportunity to do big things," Roosevelt said.

The appointment was heard as Harrison's first shot at redeeming his pledge to work for civil service reform. Roosevelt quickly showed that he would stand for neither hanky-panky nor favoritism.

"No attempt to get around the law in any way will be permitted. Democrats and Republicans alike will have fair play," he said.

To prove that he meant it, in June, 1889, Roosevelt and the two other members of his commission instituted an on-the-spot investigation of the notorious New York customhouse, with the result that three employees were charged

with laxity, negligence and fraud and summarily fired. That
done, Roosevelt turned his attention to other big cities, not
sparing even Harrison's own bailiwick, Indianapolis.

There, to what must have been the President's chagrin,
Roosevelt investigated complaints against Ben's former law
partner, William Wallace, whom Harrison had recently
appointed city postmaster. Fortunately, Wallace was not
found guilty as charged and was permitted to stay in office.
Undoubtedly Harrison wished his friend had never been
so embarrassingly put on the spot, but he really could not
fault Roosevelt for being too thorough.

Harrison could not, or would not, but other Hoosiers
were not so reticent. In fact, members of the Indianapolis
Republican Club complained so often and so publicly that
it became known as "the Kickers' Club."

In Milwaukee, the postmaster, George Paul, did not fare
so well as Wallace in Indianapolis. Roosevelt found that
Paul had used competitive examinations, but he had seen
that they were scored so that the men he wanted to reward
got the highest marks; he begged that Harrison extend Paul
no mercy.

In this manner, Roosevelt stepped on Republican toes in
state after state, and the person most blamed for the action
was Harrison himself. Congressmen, who had to answer to
the constituents in their various states, told the President
he had to do something to step on Roosevelt in turn.

By the time Congress adjourned for the summer, Harrison's party popularity had waned considerably, but he had
the sorry satisfaction of knowing that he had held to his
principles. He had promised to allow "no individuals, corporations, or communities to nullify the law"—in this case,
the Civil Service or Pendleton Act of 1883—and he had not.

He needed a vacation from the vexations of office as much
as anybody, and in July he consented to go back to Deer

Park with Carrie and the three McKees. There, regular out-
door exercise, including the hunting and fishing he had
enjoyed since boyhood, proved beneficial to his health and
spirits. He looked tanned and well as he set off for Maine to
pay a politically expedient call on Secretary of State Blaine
in August.

Harrison was enthusiastically welcomed everywhere his
train stopped en route. Blaine had told him this would be
the case in his letter of invitation.

"I have been gratified with the general, I may say the
universal, approval which your administration has thus far
received from the great mass of people who have no interest
except in wise and pure government." Until he saw it for
himself, Harrison, so criticized on all sides by politicians,
had been afraid to believe it.

Needless to say, the President returned to Washington in
a much better frame of mind than he had left it some weeks
before. He felt ready now to set into motion a much needed
program to improve United States relations with Latin
America.

Presidents Arthur and Cleveland had chosen to veto all
suggested plans for a Pan-American congress. Harrison had
realized that, and in his letter of January 17, 1889, offering
Blaine the State Secretaryship, he had said, "I am especially
interested in the improvement of our relations with Central
and South American states. We must win their confidence
by deserving it. Only men of experience, of high character,
and broad view, should be sent even to the least of them."

He and Blaine had talked over their policy for the Ameri-
cas during the spring and again during their Maine reunion.
As a result, eighteen countries had been invited to meet in
Washington in October, 1889.

Harrison and Blaine had great hopes for the Congress of
American States. They talked of a customs union, inter-
American rail and steamship lines, trademark and copy-

right laws, and arbitration treaties. Harrison in particular dreamed of the development of a large United States merchant marine so expanded trade with South America could be a reality.

The President spent much time and thought on selecting just the right delegates to represent the United States at the conference table. He wanted businessmen who were also diplomats, men who had high reputations for personal integrity. He didn't care about their political persuasion, nor from which section of the country they came, just so they answered his criteria.

The first event of the Congress of American States was a noon reception at the White House on October 2. The delegates paraded in two-by-two, to the music of John Phillip Sousa and his Marine Band. The renowned band played the national airs of all the countries before lunch. That this compliment was appreciated was obvious from the conversation during the meal. Harrison, withdrawing afterwards so the first preliminary session could begin, pronounced himself well pleased with the amicable way things were going.

A six-weeks' tour through the northern and midwestern states was the next thing planned for the delegates. The idea was to acquaint them with our manufactures, agricultural products, and our military resources and to show them that the United States was well worth trading with.

In mid-November the conference delegates returned to Washington and business sessions began. They continued until mid-April, 1890, and Blaine reported to Harrison that it was amazing how conciliatory the attitude of the delegates was, despite contrasts in temperament, language, and custom.

Harrison's farewell to the delegates brought him, as he said, both pain and pleasure.

"I participate in the regret which the delegates from the

United States feel who are to part with those from other countries. I take pleasure in the knowledge that your labors have been brought to a happy conclusion. . . . I bid each of you a heartfelt goodbye."

Newspapers all over the United States generally agreed that the conference had served a most important purpose. The New York *Herald* said, "From this day the Monroe Doctrine passes into a stage of higher development." The New York *Tribune* declared, "The ground has been leveled, the way has been opened for securing united action on the part of the eighteen commonwealths, action which will promote the enlightened self-interest of each and the common welfare of all. It now remains for the United States to take the initiative and to complete a great work of high civilization."

The Congress of American States had been only one of the things to occupy Harrison's attention in the fall of 1889. He had also been busy with the preparation of his first Annual Message to Congress. He signed the proclamation that would admit four new states—Montana, Washington, and the Dakotas—into the Union. He met regularly with his Cabinet. In addition, he was much concerned with illness in his "official family," for when his secretary, E. W. Halford, collapsed at his desk and had to be hospitalized, Harrison spent hours at his bedside trying to comfort the stricken man.

Most of Harrison's time was given over to the Annual Message, for not only Congress but the nation was waiting to hear what he would say. He knew it would have to be a strong message, covering everything of moment.

One thing that worried Harrison particularly was the outcome of the Free Silver Convention, meeting in St. Louis. The convention was composed of delegates from the Southern Farmers' Alliance and the Northern Farmers' Al-

liance: five million men with one main aim. They wanted
the Coinage Act of 1873, forbidding the coinage of silver
dollars and placing the country on a gold basis, repealed and
the *free and unlimited coinage of silver* at the ratio of sixteen ounces of silver to one ounce of gold restored. Their
argument was that the deflation that had cost the farmer so
much could be reversed by this process.

Harrison was aware that the farmers' strength, potent
enough already, would be much increased by the addition of
the four new states. Their pressure on the new Congress
could in fact be formidable. Moreover, the alliances had
threatened to form a new political party. If they did, the
Republican party would lose more from its ranks than the
Democrats.

The President finished drafting his message over Thanks-
giving weekend, 1889, and on Monday, December 2, sent it
to the Government Printing Office. He gave orders that it
was *not* to be released to the press in advance of its reading
to Congress the following day. He didn't want its impact
lessened.

The message commenced with a reminder that representatives of the independent states of North and South America were even then gathered in earnest conference in
Washington and held out assurance that only good results
could flow from so auspicious a meeting. It next touched
on other aspects of the Administration's foreign policy and
then prepared deftly for discussion of domestic affairs by
saying, "Within our borders a general condition of prosperity prevails. The harvests of last summer were excep-
tionally abundant, and the trade conditions now prevailing
seem to promise a successful season to the merchants and
the manufacturers and general employment to our working
people."

He followed that general laudatory comment with specific statements. He did not shrink from the silver question; indeed, he proclaimed himself a "friend of silver," with the comment: "I have always been an advocate of the use of silver in our currency. We are large producers of that metal and should not discredit it." But immediately afterwards he warned against the free coinage of the metal, saying that it would be "discreditable to our financial management and disastrous to all business interests." He added that any safe legislation upon the subject *must* secure the *equality* of gold and silver coins in their commercial uses.

Passing from the silver question to other items of national interest, he made strong recommendations for new laws in regard to veterans' pensions, civil rights, and labor conditions. He told what each department under the control of his Cabinet members had accomplished and what was pending, going into detail about everything from the treatment of Indian tribes to the desperate need for a new navy, a new merchant marine, and stronger coastal defenses.

The President had, in fact, touched on every conceivable area of executive concern in his message, and it would take some time for its content to be digested. But both early and late comments on it were largely complimentary, and there was no doubt that nationally it had aroused both interest and admiration.

Most gratifying of all to Ben was the reaction in Indianapolis, where he had been more often criticized than praised in recent months. Said the Indianapolis *News:* "No state paper published at any time within the past twenty-five years has been greeted so favorably by the Indianapolis reading public as this masterful message of President Harrison."

CHAPTER 13

Thorny Problems

THE YEAR 1890 began, as usual for the Harrisons, with a late morning reception on New Year's Day. Ben and Carrie had initiated the custom early in their Indianapolis days. They saw no reason to change it because they were the First Family of the land.

In the White House, of course, the guests were more celebrated than in Indianapolis, and the press coverage was more elaborate. Reporters for the Indianapolis papers, knowing that the home folks would be interested in every detail, recorded the events of the day fully. At breakfast the next day, Hoosiers could "see" the whole picture, from the moment the Marine Band struck up "Hail to the Chief," through three hours of handshakes with "brave men and fair women, gay uniforms and rich toilets," to the time when the doors were finally locked and the family could sit down to lunch.

But the year that started so favorably soon saw sorrowing faces in the Harrison official family. On January 15, James Blaine's brilliant son, Walker, suddenly died, to be followed a few days later by his daughter, Alice.

"I fear for the result on Mr. Blaine," Harrison said.

He had good reason to fear, because James Blaine himself had been ailing often of late. Many times Harrison had been obliged to fill in for his Secretary of State at important foreign policy meetings, and he had begun to wonder if he should begin to look for another secretary.

National problems too now began to develop at a great rate, some little, some large. One of the former would have made William Henry Harrison feel right at home, for it concerned incidents with Indians. Navajos and Cherokees were both claiming that their reservations were not adequate for their needs, and they had begun living beyond the reservation boundaries. Benjamin Harrison was not his grandfather, however, and he turned this matter over to the Secretary of the Interior. He himself had to deal with more wide-reaching questions.

Most thorny among these were what to do about (1) protecting Negro civil rights, (2) providing pensions for veterans, (3) dealing with trusts and monopolies, (4) settling the matter of silver coinage, and (5) providing new tariff legislation.

To act on any of these, Harrison needed congressional assistance. On the surface it would seem that he should have no trouble, because the Fifty-first Congress was controlled by men of his own party. The fact was, however, that the leaders of both houses were unsympathetic to the President. They were more liberal Blaine men through and through, even to being "men from Maine" themselves. The leader of the Senate was Eugene Hale. The Speaker of the House of Representatives was Thomas B. Reed.

By tradition, the Speaker—the presiding officer of the House—was given almost autocratic powers. He himself was chairman of the Committee on Rules, and he appointed all standing committees. Reed had appointed other "men from Maine" to head up all of these that mattered. Most notable were Nelson Dingley of the Ways and Means Committee and Charles Boutelle of the Committee on Naval Affairs. It was no wonder historians were later to say the

Harrison administration might well be called the Maine administration. Even the Chief Justice of the United States Supreme Court, Melville Fuller, was from that state.

President Harrison could not help knowing what opposition he was up against, but that did not stop him from earnestly recommending constructive legislation on all national problems.

The matter of votes for Negroes supposedly had been provided for by the Fifteenth Amendment, which had become law in 1868. However, it was a fact that in the South Negroes were being deprived of their constitutional rights, and this Harrison, the Constitutional President, could not tolerate. He said to the Congress:

> It has been the hope of every patriot that a sense of justice and respect for the law would work a gradual cure of these flagrant evils . . . but when in fact is the black man to have those full civil rights which have so long been his in law?
>
> I earnestly invoke your attention to the consideration of such measures as are within your well-defined constitutional powers to secure to *all* our people *a free exercise of the rights of suffrage and every other civil right* under the Constitution and laws of the United States.

He went on to ask that the supervision of elections as was already provided for by law be increased and strengthened, and in addition to secure that

> the colored man should be protected in all of his relations to the Federal Government, whether as litigant, juror, or witness in our courts, as an elector for members of Congress, or as a peaceful traveler upon our interstate railways.

These requests for honest elections and fair play were praised by ministers, educators, and many influential northern whites. Also Harrison received heavy mail from Negroes in both North and South.

The representatives of these people who endorsed Harrison's policy so forcibly could not ignore the clear mandate even if they wanted to. Accordingly, several election bills were introduced in both houses of Congress, by such stalwart Republicans as Senators John Sherman and George Hoar and Representative Henry Cabot Lodge. Since the bills had many similarities, their authors agreed they should be edited and combined into one bill. This, known as the Force Bill, provided for supervision of federal elections by the national government. Henry Cabot Lodge introduced it in the House on June 19, 1890. It passed without alteration on July 2. It was then sent to the Senate.

Harrison was pleased and encouraged by the seeming ease with which the Force Bill had gone through the House, although having sat in Congress himself he knew how firm a hand Speaker Thomas Reed must have kept on the controls.

July 2 was an important day for the President for another reason, too. On that date he signed into law the Sherman Anti-Trust Act, the first national one of its kind.

The public had long wanted government regulation of business practices. The establishment of the first industrial combination, the Standard Oil trust, in 1878 had been followed by other large combinations controlling such commodities as whiskey, sugar, lead, and beef. Trying to protect themselves, many western and southern states had enacted their own antitrust laws. But they were useless for dealings in interstate commerce. Only federal government legislation could control that.

This problem, too, Harrison had studied and then put in congressional hands, saying, "Earnest attention must be given to a consideration of the restraint of those combinations of capital called 'trusts.' When organized, as they often are, to crush out all healthy competition and to monopolize the production or sale of an article of commerce and general necessity, they are *dangerous conspiracies* against the public good."

Consideration was given to the matter by the Senate Judiciary Committee, and the result was the act named for Senator John Sherman. It consisted of eight major provisions, but the gist was that "Every contract, combination in the form of trust or otherwise, or conspiracy in restraint of commerce among the several states or with foreign nations, is hereby declared *illegal*."

The act further authorized the federal government to proceed against a trust to dissolve it and invested federal circuit courts with the power to prevent and restrain violations of the law.

This act is still on the statute books substantially as passed that July of 1890, although its somewhat "cloudy" phrasing was clarified and strengthened by the Clayton Act of 1914.

The passing in June, 1890, of an act to take care of disabled veterans had given Harrison more personal satisfaction than the Anti-Trust Bill. Known as the Dependent Pension Act, it granted pensions to veterans of the Union forces with at least ninety days of service who were then or thereafter disabled and so could not earn a livelihood by manual labor. The former Civil War general had had the old soldiers much on his mind, and he was glad to be able to discharge the nation's debt to them in such a satisfactory way.

By Independence Day, 1890, President Harrison could count three of the five thorniest questions of the year as satisfactorily settled. Still left were the problems of silver coinage and tariff legislation, but Harrison felt justified in taking a short vacation anyway. He joined his family at Cape May, New Jersey, in the cottage his Postmaster General, John Wanamaker, had offered to Mrs. Harrison.

At Cape May the President was able to breathe the sea breezes, but he could not escape his problems. Secretary of State Blaine, for one, would not let him. Blaine came to New Jersey to protest one part of the tariff bill being sponsored in Congress by William McKinley.

His objection was to the provision that sugar—raw sugar —be placed on the free list. The reason for tariff revision was to cut down on revenue and thus to lessen the surplus in the national treasury. Since sugar imports had paid duties of $50,000,000 annually, making sugar duty free would naturally cut the surplus considerably.

Harrison tried to explain the sense of this to Blaine, but Blaine would not listen. Too many Latin American imports were already being admitted free, Blaine said, while many American *exports* carried high duties. This, he insisted, was unfair.

While Blaine and Harrison were still discussing the matter, they learned that the McKinley Bill had been passed by the House of Representatives. This meant it was too late to do anything to stop the free sugar provision, so Harrison promised Blaine he would "recommend an amendment to provide for the reimposing of duties if other nations withheld reciprocal advantages."

The threat to veto the McKinley Bill had been used to advantage by free silver advocates in the House. Using "you scratch my back and I'll scratch yours" tactics, western representatives voted into office by the Farmers' Alliances were able to wrest concessions from gold standard easterners. The result was the Sherman Silver Purchase Act, passed on July 14.

This represented, really, a compromise, not a victory for the silverites. It did not provide for free coinage of silver, but it did require the treasury to purchase 4,500,000 ounces of silver each month at the prevailing market price. It further required the treasury to issue treasury notes redeemable in gold or silver in payment for the silver.

The mutual back-scratching method worked, for both measures eventually passed Congress, though the McKinley Bill took weeks of further debate and had hundreds of amendments before the legislators would agree upon it.

All this talk, debate, and dissension had kept the Fifty-first Congress in session many more months than usual, but it was finally ready to adjourn on October 1, 1890.

Shortly after lunch on that day, President Harrison appeared to sign the tariff bill and other less momentous measures. An almost holiday mood prevailed, and leaders of both parties came to shake Harrison's hand and assure him that the session had been extremely worthwhile. Whether or not all the 1,985 bills they had passed would indeed prove to be that, the session had certainly been a busy one. Congress had acted on all the thorny problems the President had sent it. How the public would react to the solutions the legislators had come up with was likely to show up in the approaching off-year elections.

Since he had been successful in getting his program through Congress, thereby keeping his pre-election promises, Harrison felt cautiously optimistic about public reaction. Republican party men across the country, however, had heard mutterings they did not like. They hastened to still these by issuing millions of pamphlets blowing the Grand Old Party's horn.

"Facts From the Treasury," for instance, boasted that the G.O.P. administration had saved the people no less than $51 million on its redemption of bonded debts.

"Better Days for Farmers" assured that sector of the population that the McKinley tariff would help, not hurt, agriculture—without raising prices or increasing the cost of living.

The Democrats, not surprisingly, moved heaven and earth to offset these glowing statements. In order to prove that the Republicans were liars, they themselves manipulated prices, sometimes pushing up the cost on ordinary items as much as twenty times.

They were helped out by nature. In the midwest, torrential rains fell day after day, rotting many crops before they could be harvested. Since the farmers could not realize money on their produce, they could not pay off mortgages on their farms. Holders of the mortgages foreclosed, and there was widespread discontent and hardship.

As always when people are discontented, they wanted someone or something to blame. The current government made an easy target, the ballot a convenient weapon.

The result was disaster for national Republican candidates. They lost control of the House of Representatives. They kept control of the Senate by only a narrow majority. Even more significant, William McKinley was among the representatives removed from office.

President Harrison, of course, was disappointed, but he was also philosophical. Reviewing history, he noted that the same thing had happened often in midstream between presidential terms.

Two international incidents cropped up soon after the election, both serious enough to monopolize both the President's and the State Department's attention. One concerned Italy, the other Chile.

The first one arose after a multitude of little incidents between Italian immigrants and native Americans residing in New Orleans. Many of the Italians, it was known, were members of the Mafia Black Hand Society, an organization of criminals. Their "hand" was recognized as having committed many crimes in the Louisiana city, but for years fear had kept the law enforcement officers from trying to track down those who were guilty. Finally, David C. Hennessey, the chief of police, determined to end the reign-of terror. He collected enough evidence to convict and make the conviction stick—but on October 15, before he could testify before the grand jury, *he* was murdered.

Hennessey's murder was the last straw for the terrified residents of New Orleans. They formed a citizens' committee pledged to the total annihilation of the Mafia in their city. They seized many suspects, who were questioned and released. Nineteen were finally brought to trial—but for lack of evidence were found not guilty.

This was declared a failure of justice by the aroused people, and eight thousand of them stormed the prison and managed to shoot down or hang eleven of the prisoners. The other eight escaped.

The Italian government called "Outrage!" The Italian minister to the United States wanted to know what the United States was going to do about it. The problem should have been handled by Secretary of State Blaine, but Blaine was once again too ill. Harrison took the duty on himself.

He was well aware that the federal government was not empowered to interfere with an affair that had been wholly within the state of Louisiana. All he could do was suggest and request.

So that Blaine would not feel he had been passed over, Harrison went to his bedside and there dictated a telegram to Governor Nichols of Louisiana. In it, he deplored the massacre and asked that state officials do everything possible to protect the rights of Italians in New Orleans, to prevent further bloodshed, and to bring to justice those responsible for the sorry deed.

Italy, however, had no understanding of the division of power between state and federal government that had been laid down in the Constitution. She wanted full and prompt justice, and threatened that if it was not soon forthcoming, Italy would "speak with the voice of her guns." In the meantime, the Italian minister was recalled to Rome.

Harrison at once brought Albert Porter, American minister to Italy, home too. And that was the way matters stood in December, 1891, when the President had to deliver his third Annual Message to Congress. He therefore thought it advisable to suggest that Congress "make offenses against the treaty rights of foreigners domiciled in the United States cognizable in the federal courts"—in other words, make such a situation with a foreign power legally part of *national* responsibility, and within the jurisdiction of a federal court.

The Louisiana government failed to act, but luckily time began to make the incident seem less important to the Italian government. Italy, in fact, indicated she wanted to resume diplomatic relations but couldn't quite bring herself to the point of saying so.

Harrison and Blaine, conferring, decided to ease the way for her and soothe the conscience of the United States at the same time by offering King Umberto $25,000. Rather than wait for the Congress to vote the amount, they took the money from the State Department emergency fund.

Congress did not like being bypassed, but King Umberto accepted the indemnity and in April, 1892, ordered the resumption of full relations between his country and the United States.

The second international incident had been touched off during the Chilean revolution of 1891. The Chilean rebel ship, *Itata,* had been seized by American naval personnel off San Diego, because it was known to have picked up munitions of war somewhere close by. The excuse had been "possible violation of American neutrality," but it was soon discovered that, though the ship had indeed picked up arms, they had been acquired outside United States territorial waters. The *Itata* was then released, but Chilean resentment toward the United States was aroused.

The resentment broke out actively in October, when a group of American seamen in Valparaiso, Chile, was attacked by a mob, and two of them were killed. Now it was the United States' turn to be aroused, and the U.S. press demanded immediate reprisal by the State Department. Once again, Blaine was ill, and this time Harrison didn't try to work through him at all. Instead he directed the Acting Secretary, Joseph Wharton, to send a sharp note to Chile, demanding an apology and punishment for the murderers.

A half-hearted apology came, and with it the equally unsatisfactory knowledge that trial would be held "in due time."

In that same message to Congress in December, 1891, when he spoke of the Italian blow-up, Harrison said:

> This government is now awaiting the result of an investigation which is being conducted by the criminal court at Valparaiso. . . . It is expected that the result will soon be communicated to this government, together with some adequate and satisfactory response to the note by which the attention of Chile was called to this incident. *If* these expectations should be disappointed, or *if* further needless delay intervene, I will . . . bring this matter again to the attention of Congress *for such action as may be necessary*.

His "expectations" were not only disappointed, but on January 20, 1892, Chile asked that the U.S. minister to Chile be recalled.

This further slap at the United States really aroused Harrison's fighting blood. He sent an ultimatum to the Chilean government, giving the country five days to reconsider and to offer proper indemnity, or the United States would declare war.

The governments of France, Germany, and Great Britain made haste to let Chile know they would not come to her aid if she went to war with the United States. That, plus the fact that Chile knew the United States did not threaten idly, made the South American country back down in a hurry. Less than twenty-four hours after Harrison's ultimatum, Chile apologized and offered as indemnity $75,000. When the $75,000 arrived from Chile, President Harrison directed that the money be distributed among the injured sailors and the families of those who had died in Valparaiso.

The nation expressed universal satisfaction with what Theodore Roosevelt called Harrison's "timely display of firmness." The consensus was, there need be no war with foreign powers if the government would always be "prompt, vigorous, and preemptory in demanding that our flag and uniform shall always and everywhere be respected."

The only person who did not seem pleased with Harrison's handling of the Chile situation was Blaine. Ill or not, he was still Secretary of State, and he didn't want anyone to forget it.

CHAPTER **14**

Last Years

RUMORS OF ILL-FEELING between President Harrison and his Secretary of State aroused concern in some circles, joy in others, for it was again a presidential year.

Harrison himself had not made up his mind whether or not he would run for the Presidency again. He did not really want to, and yet he was reluctant to close the door to the possibility, just when he seemed finally to have gained the support and favor of men who had formerly opposed him.

One such man was the eminent reformer Benjamin Bristow. Bristow had been wavering for some time, but after the Chile affair he settled firmly in the President's camp. He said loudly that Harrison was entitled to "the confidence and support of all who put the desire for good government and national prosperity ahead of every other consideration in the selection of a Chief Executive."

This was a slap at the many politicians who wanted a glad-hander, a soft-soaper, a patronage-giver in the White House. They had never forgiven Harrison for saying he was going to "drive the elephant"—and doing it. Boss Quay of Philadelphia and Boss Platt of New York were two of these. James Blaine was their type of man.

They were not unaware that Blaine had been ill often during the past four years. Certain newspapers had seemed to relish playing up the fact, particularly the New York

Herald. In headlines it had asked: IS BLAINE'S MIND GIVING
WAY? and, BLAINE'S BREAKING DOWN, THOUGH FRIENDS DENY
IT.

Harrison, who knew the real state of Blaine's health, tried
to be as consoling as possible. After one of the *Herald*'s
crepe-hanging stories had appeared, the President wrote the
Secretary of State, saying: "The over-readiness of the newspapers to kill off public men is one of the curious and discreditable phases of modern journalism."

Blaine eventually believed that Harrison honestly had
nothing but good will toward him, and so their personal
relationship improved. But Mrs. Blaine had let what she
thought of as Harrison's slights build up in her mind until
she felt great, even vengeful bitterness toward him.

In the spring of 1892, Blaine's health did seem better,
but he would not commit himself on the subject of the
greatest importance for the Republican Convention. Republicans who were dissatisfied with Harrison were content
enough to have it that way for the time being. As long as
Blaine didn't express his desires, he could be used as a bargaining threat—or at least that was their hope.

They were, of course, wrong. Benjamin Harrison was not
a bargainer. Moreover, in April, 1892, he was so personally
upset that he didn't want to be approached about anything
except matters of immediate national concern. His beloved
Carrie was bedridden with what doctors called nervous
prostration, and he spent hours at her bedside.

The Republican Convention was scheduled to be held
early in June, and Harrison's most loyal friends and boosters felt that he must make a definite statement. They begged
him to announce that he would be a candidate to succeed
himself, so that they could work actively for him. They
warned that already "hostile delegations" were being
chosen by "malcontents." These included not only the

disappointed patronage-seeking bosses, Quay and Platt, but also the new National Chairman of the Republican Party, James S. Clarkson.

Harrison only repeated what he had said before: "If a renomination has to be schemed for by me, it is, first, pretty clear evidence that it ought not to come to me; and, second, that it offers rather a discouraging prospect for success."

The pro-Harrison newspapers did not like this do-nothing policy; yet their hands were all but tied. The farthest they dared go was, as the owner of the New York *Tribune,* Whitelaw Reid, admitted, "discreetly to do the right thing by Harrison and the administration."

The anti-Harrison forces felt no compulsion to be discreet, but they were not united behind one man, either. Some wanted Blaine, some favored William McKinley. Blaine had the most followers, and they chose to blind themselves to the fact that he was far from a well man. They romanticized him, seeing him as he used to be, the plumed knight who could carry their banner to victory.

The surest indication that Blaine was not well was the fact that he allowed untrue things to be said about Harrison without objecting. Honesty and graciousness combined had hitherto been his character trademarks. Moreover, active or not, he was still Harrison's Secretary of State and should have insisted on respect being maintained for his Chief.

Blaine's acquiescence encouraged his supporters to multiply the viciousness of their attacks on Harrison's character, until finally in mid-May the President felt that not only his image but that of the nation had been besmirched. This he could not allow, so he announced in ringing tones:

"No Harrison has ever retreated in the presence of a foe without giving battle, and so I have determined to stand and fight."

Now at last the Harrison supporters could go full steam

ahead, and they did. They were careful to stick to the truth, because they knew Harrison would not have tolerated anything else, but they made the truth tell. For instance, they repeatedly stressed the President's great physical strength, firm military carriage, ruddy manly complexion, as contrasted to Blaine's "flabby wrinkled face and form bent as he walked." They pointed out how many foreign policy moves Harrison had been obliged to make because Blaine was unable to act. And of course they pictured him as the ideal Republican—the true friend of the high protective tariff, the staunch supporter of bimetallism (the use of both gold and silver as the standard of value), the soldiers' advocate.

Through all this, Harrison and Blaine continued to confront each other at Cabinet meetings. Harrison would not ask for Blaine's resignation, and it apparently did not occur to Blaine that he should resign. This, too, would later be pointed at as evidence that the Secretary's mind was not alert. Finally, Blaine's son Emmons told him he simply could not remain a member of the President's official family, and on June 4, 1892, he did bow out.

The Republican Convention opened in Minneapolis three days later. The big wheels of the party had, of course, been on hand a good week previous to it, and the strength of the candidates had been pretty well sized up by Harrison men. As they saw it, the Blaine boom was not going to be much more than a pop, but the McKinley power might prove troublesome. The thing to do was insure that Harrison was nominated on the first roll call of the states—and the way to do it was to see that McKinley was made Permanent Chairman of the Convention. In that role, having to do distasteful things like stop demonstrations, make rules, and such, he hopefully would annoy people so they'd think twice about him as a candidate.

All proceeded as the Harrison men wished. On June 10, the names of candidates were presented: Harrison, Blaine, McKinley, Thomas B. Reed, Robert T. Lincoln, and several favorite sons. On June 11, the balloting began. The only surprise was that when Ohio's votes were cast, McKinley himself said he wanted to be "recorded for Harrison."

There really was no contest. Harrison won renomination by the time the state of Texas was first called to cast its votes. The next day, Whitelaw Reid was acclaimed for second place on the ticket, the Convention having believed Levi Morton, who once had said he did not wish to succeed himself as Vice-president.

On June 22, the Democratic National Convention, meeting in Chicago, nominated Grover Cleveland for President again. Countering the Republican Party's chief promise— to maintain a high protective tariff—the Democrats declared that "the federal government has no constitutional power to impose and collect tariff duties except for purposes of revenue."

Both major parties had now spoken. They had given the voters of the nation candidates who had already demonstrated how they would act in the Presidency. And it seemed the voters didn't much care which one got the nod this time.

"It will take a bomb to excite the people," was the complaint on both sides of the political fence.

The bomb was provided by labor disturbances. At the Carnegie Steel Company plant in Homestead, Pennsylvania, violence flared after failure of management to agree on a new wage scale. In an attempt to break the grip of the steelworkers union, the company employed Pinkerton detectives as strikebreakers. In desperation the strikers fired on and killed several Pinkerton men. The state militia had to be summoned to restore order, and finally the strike was called off.

Similarly, in riots at a silver mine in Idaho, troops were called in to help. This time they were federal soldiers, as requested by the governor.

Harrison was criticized for sending them. In answer, he repeated what he had said often before. "Obedience to law must be respected in all disputes."

The Chicago *Tribune* trumpeted its admiration for the "fearless President," who acted without regard to the fact that his party might lose votes thereby.

Evidence that this might indeed be the case began to disturb Republican leaders. They urged Harrison to make personal appearances in at least a few doubtful states. Friendly, unrehearsed talks such as he had given from his front porch during the last campaign, they said, would remind people that he was a fatherly figure, not a military tyrant.

But as the summer drew to a close, Harrison was too worried about his beloved Carrie to spare any thought for political popularity. She was a victim of tuberculosis and was not expected to live much longer. He spent night after sleepless night watching at her bedside, not wanting to chance being away if she should call for him.

She died on the morning of October 25, 1892. Her husband accompanied her coffin to Indianapolis, where she was laid to rest in Crown Hill cemetery.

After that blow, nothing else held much meaning for Harrison. Even when he learned that Cleveland had defeated him for the Presidency, he was too numb to feel any hurt.

"Political defeat carries no personal grief," he said.

The professional politicians of his party could not accept the beating so philosophically. They held many post mortems to determine the cause. Basic to it, they decided, was the "orneryness of the employee class," which voted against their employers out of "pure cussedness."

Told this, the President shrugged and agreed. In picture-esque language, he acknowledged the people's repudiation of the high protective tariff as well.

"The workingman declined to walk under the protective umbrella because it sheltered his employer, too."

Christmas was very quiet in the White House that year, and so was New Year's Day, 1893. No reception was held, since official Washington was all in mourning for Mrs. Harrison.

January saw the death of James Blaine, too, an occasion of fresh grief to Harrison, who had loved his Secretary of State even when sorely tried by him.

Then something happened that perked up Harrison's spirits a bit. Hawaii's Queen Liliuokalani, who when ascending the throne in 1891 had renounced the pro-American constitution of 1887, was overthrown by subjects who objected to her autocratic rule. United States minister John L. Stevens asked that Marines be sent to protect American lives and property. Further, without authorization from the State Department, Stevens recognized the self-appointed president of Hawaii, Sanford Dole, an American planter. Together, Stevens and Dole declared the islands an American protectorate and drew up a treaty of annexation.

Harrison did not approve of revolutions, but he did believe that, since one had occurred, steps had to be taken to assure that no foreign power would secure Hawaii. On February 15, he sent the treaty to the Senate with a covering letter. He reminded the senators that

It has been the policy of this administration not only to respect but to encourage the continuance of an independent government in the Hawaiian Islands, so long as it afforded suitable guarantees for the protection of life and property, and maintained a stability and strength that gave adequate security against the domination of any power. . . .

It is now evident that the monarchy had become effete and the Queen's government so weak and inadequate as to be the prey of designing and unscrupulous persons.

He went on to say that the Queen's restoration was undesirable, and that, as he saw it, only two courses were advisable: one, the establishment of a protectorate by the United States; the other, annexation as a territory. He advocated the latter, which was laid out in the treaty that was before the Senate.

- Harrison hoped for "full and prompt affirmative action" on the part of the Senate, but Democratic and anti-imperialist Republican opposition delayed ratification of the treaty. Hawaii was not to be annexed to the United States until June, 1900, when McKinley was President.

Taking the Hawaiian treaty to the Senate was one of Harrison's last acts as President. On March 4, he handed the reins of government once more to Grover Cleveland. That same evening, he left by train for Indianapolis.

He had dreaded returning home without his beloved Carrie, but waiting for him at his North Delaware Street house were his daughter, Mamie McKee, and his grandchildren, Mary and Benjamin ("Baby"), and so the dreadful moment was made less dreadful.

Harrison returned to the practice of law, too, but in a limited way. He preferred to spend his time writing about his views. He completed many magazine articles—nine appeared in *The Ladies' Home Journal*—and a book, *This Country of Ours*.

He returned also to the church and charitable work he had so enjoyed in his years as a private citizen, accepted a national office in the Presbyterian Church, and sat on the advisory board of the Indianapolis Orphan Asylum.

In late 1895, having been a widower for three years,

Benjamin Harrison proposed to Mary Lord Dimmick, a widow much younger than his sixty-two years. They announced their intentions during the Christmas season and were married in April, 1896. Ten months later, a daughter, Elizabeth, was born to them.

Even before his remarriage, Republican friends who saw him reported that "due to love or something else," Harrison was "much more approachable" than he had been before. This kind of talk was easily translated as meaning Harrison would be willing to consider another term in the Presidency. This he explicitly denied, first in a letter to the Chairman of the Indiana Republican Committee, and again in a letter to a too-eager booster two weeks later. He said that he thought a "fresh pilot could steer the Ship of State more satisfactorily," and let it be known that he personally favored Iowa senator William B. Allison.

Allison did not get the nod at the June Republican Nominating Convention. William McKinley did. The platform adopted, however, was one Harrison thoroughly approved: again the high protective tariff, but in addition a vigorous foreign policy that included annexation of the Hawaiian Islands.

The last years of Harrison's life paralleled McKinley's in the White House. He continued to hold aloof from national politics, choosing instead to stick to law. But in that field he reaped new laurels, and in 1899 was asked by the Venezuelan government to be its chief counsel in a boundary dispute with Great Britain.

Harrison gave all he had to the Venezuelan case, working as he used to do when a young man, from sunup to sundown every day but Sunday. In the end, he appeared at an arbitration tribunal in Paris, where in October, 1899, he delivered a twenty-five-hour-long closing argument. The verdict, when given, was not all he had hoped, but neither was it what Great Britain wanted. He said simply, "It could have been worse," and would not comment when the newspapers screamed "double dealing" on the part of Great Britain.

In the following year Harrison argued some important cases in the Indiana Supreme Court, where he had once served as reporter, and also in the Supreme Court of the United States, but he let it be known that he would no longer be a slave to his profession. Perhaps he was feeling the weight of his years, though he was only sixty-seven. Perhaps he just wanted to enjoy life with his young wife and little daughter.

He did not have much time to enjoy leisure. In the late winter of 1901 he contracted pneumonia. On March 13, he died.

His body was placed on a bier in the State House. On Saturday, March 16, thousands of Indiana soldiers, led by remnants of the regiment which had followed Harrison to war, paraded solemnly past it. Some spoke of Little Ben, remembering how he had said "Come on, boys!" and charged into the fray. Many said prayers.

Eulogies spoken at Harrison's funeral in the First Presbyterian Church next day were more flowery than the soldiers' reminiscences, but none of them would have pleased Ben as much as the tribute from his "boys."

What kind of man was Benjamin Harrison? The basis of his character was an instinct to do the polite, honest, dignified thing in every contingency. He never compromised with the truth. He represented a decency and dignity above his party and above his time. For this he was reviled by the very men who should have honored him: the high priests of the Republican temple.

What kind of Chief Executive was he? He was a strictly constitutional President. The Constitution and its amendments were his yardstick for everything he did and said during his White House years. For this, too, he was criticized by the high priests of his party.

How did the people judge him during his lifetime? Perhaps they did not love him, because he would not flatter them by pretending their judgment was infallible. But they trusted him. He never told them anything just to get their votes. He never deceived them with promises he did not expect to keep.

How does history judge Benjamin Harrison? Not as wisely as it will. From the day of his inauguration as President of the United States, he lived the part. He brought immense dignity to the office.

The same cannot be said of all men who, like Harrison, were crowned with the highest honor our land can bestow.

Bibliography

American Heritage Pictorial History of the Presidents, Vol. 2. New York: American Heritage Publishing Co., 1968.

Andrist, Ralph K. *Making of the Nation.* New York: American Heritage Publishing Co., 1968.

Copeland, Thomas Campbell. *Harrison and Reid.* New York: Charles L. Webster Company, 1892.

Goebel, Dorothy B., and Goebel, Julius. *Generals in the White House.* New York: Doubleday, Doran and Co., Inc., 1945.

Harney, Gilbert L. *Lives of Benjamin Harrison and Levi P. Morton.* Providence, R. I.: J. A. and R. A. Reid, Publishers, 1888.

Harrison, Benjamin. *Public Papers and Addresses.* Washington, D.C.: Government Printing Office, 1893.

_____. *Views of an Ex-President.* Indianapolis: Bowen-Merrill, 1901.

Northrup, Henry D. *Life and Public Services of Benjamin Harrison.* Columbus, Ohio: Wabash Publishing Co., 1892.

Sievers, Harry J. *Benjamin Harrison, Hoosier President.* Indianapolis: Bobbs-Merrill Co., Inc., 1968.

_____. *Benjamin Harrison, Hoosier Statesman.* New York: University Publishers, Inc., 1958.

_____. *Benjamin Harrison, Hoosier Warrior.* New York: University Publishers, Inc., 1952.

Stoddard, Henry L. *As I Knew Them*. New York: Harper and Brothers Publishers, 1927.

Stone, Irving. *They Also Ran*. New York: New American Library, 1968.

Taussig, F. W. *Tariff History of the United States*. New York: G. P. Putnam's Sons, 1923.

Volweiler, Albert T., (Ed.), *Correspondence Between Benjamin Harrison and James G. Blaine*. Philadelphia: American Philosophical Society, 1940.

Wallace, Lew. *Life of General Ben Harrison*. Philadelphia: Hubbard Bros., Publishers, 1888.

White, William Allen. *Masks in a Pageant*. New York: The Macmillan Co., 1928.

Index